Great Games for
CITY KIDS

ZONDERVAN/YOUTH SPECIALTIES BOOKS

Adventure Games
Amazing Tension Getters
ArtSource™ Volume 1—Fantastic Activities
ArtSource™ Volume 2—Borders, Symbols, Holidays, and Attention Getters
ArtSource™ Volume 3—Sports
ArtSource™ Volume 4—Phrases and Verses
Attention Grabbers for 4th-6th Graders (Get 'em Growing)
Called to Care
The Complete Student Missions Handbook
Creative Socials and Special Events
Divorce Recovery for Teenagers
Feeding Your Forgotten Soul (Spiritual Growth for Youth Workers)
Get 'Em Talking
Good Clean Fun
Good Clean Fun, Volume 2
Great Games for City Kids
Great Games for 4th-6th Graders (Get 'em Growing)
Great Ideas for Small Youth Groups
Greatest Skits on Earth
Greatest Skits on Earth, Volume 2
Growing Up in America
High School Ministry
High School TalkSheets
Holiday Ideas for Youth Groups (Revised Edition)
Hot Talks
How to Survive Middle School (Get 'em Growing)
Ideas for Social Action
Incredible Stories (Get 'em Growing)
Intensive Care: Helping Teenagers in Crisis
Junior High Game Nights
Junior High Ministry
Junior High TalkSheets
The Ministry of Nurture
More Attention Grabbers for 4th-6th Graders (Get 'em Growing)
More Great Games for 4th-6th Graders (Get 'em Growing)
More Quick and Easy Activities for 4th-6th Graders (Get 'em Growing)
On-Site: 40 On-Location Youth Programs
Option Plays
Organizing Your Youth Ministry
Play It! Great Games for Groups
Quick and Easy Activities for 4th-6th Graders (Get 'em Growing)
Rock Talk
Super Sketches for Youth Ministry
Teaching the Bible Creatively
Teaching the Truth about Sex
Tension Getters
Tension Getters Two
Unsung Heroes: How to Recruit and Train Volunteer Youth Workers
Up Close and Personal: How to Build Community in Your Youth Group
Youth Ministry Nuts and Bolts
The Youth Specialties Handbook for Great Camps and Retreats
Youth Specialties Clip Art Book
Youth Specialties Clip Art Book, Volume 2

Great Games for CITY KIDS

Over 200 Games and Learning Activities
for Urban Youth Ministry

Nelson E. Copeland, Jr.

Youth Specialties

Zondervan Publishing House
A Division of HarperCollinsPublishers

Great Games for City Kids

Copyright © 1991 by Youth Specialties, Inc.

Youth Specialties Books, 1224 Greenfield Drive, El Cajon, California 92021, are published by Zondervan Publishing House, 1415 Lake Drive, S.E., Grand Rapids, Michigan 49506

Library of Congress Cataloging-in-Publication Data

Copeland, Nelson E., 1967—
   Great games for city kids / Nelson E. Copeland, Jr.
     p. cm.
   "Youth specialties."
   ISBN 0-310-54091-7
   1. Group games—United States. 2. Educational games—United States. I. Title.
   GV1204.12.C67 1991
   790.1—dc20   91-6542
                                                CIP

Edited by Lory Floyd and J. Cheri McLaughlin
Interior design and typography by Rogers Design & Associates
Cover designed by Michael Kern
Cover photography by Mark Rayburn and Mark Snyder

Printed in the United States of America

91 92 93 94 95 96 97 98 99 / / 10 9 8 7 6 5 4 3 2 1

About the YOUTHSOURCE™ Publishing Group

YOUTHSOURCE™ books, tapes, videos, and other resources pool the expertise of three of the finest youth ministry resource providers in the world:

• **Campus Life Books**—publishers of the award-winning *Campus Life* magazine, who for nearly fifty years have helped high schoolers live Christian lives.

•**Youth Specialties**—serving ministers to middle school, junior high, and high school youths for over twenty years through books, magazines, and training events such as the National Youth Workers Convention.

•**Zondervan Publishing House**—one of the oldest, largest, and most respected evangelical Christian publishers in the world.

Campus Life
465 Gundersen Dr.
Carol Stream, IL 60188
708/260-6200

Youth Specialties
1224 Greenfield Dr.
El Cajon, CA 92021
619/440-2333

Zondervan
1415 Lake Dr. S.E.
Grand Rapids, MI
49506 616/698-6900

To Jesus who made me.
To my mother who trained me.
To my father who directed me.
To my sister who makes me proud.
To my family who gives me dignity.

CONTENTS

PREFACE

Wow! What a great book! Nelson Copeland's *Great Games for City Kids* is going to be a real landmark on the otherwise bleak landscape of resources for urban youth ministry. This book gives us hands-on, practical ideas for recreational activities with kids in the urban setting. Youth workers will find here both games that are designed to teach and games that are just plain fun. What's more, they actually work! These games were developed on the streets and sidewalks of urban Philadelphia. The fact that Nelson Copeland is a graduate of Eastern College and a veteran youth worker with Tony Campolo's urban ministry here in Philadelphia just adds to my excitement about this book. I'm thrilled that it's been written and that Youth Specialties has the foresight to get it into the hands of youth workers.

Duffy Robbins
Chairman, Department of Youth Ministry
Eastern College

FOREWORD

An urban underclass is growing up in America, and Christian youth workers do not know how to relate to it. We go into urban settings with good intentions—and even with great commitment—but, for reasons that many of us do not understand, we do not seem to make much headway.

The two major parachurch youth movements in America have made Herculean efforts to reach out into this urban underclass and give these kids the Gospel of Christ. But those who serve in the cities of America under the auspices of Young Life and Youth for Christ would be the first to admit that they have yet to get a handle on how to be effective. Oh, they have had their successes. There are hundreds of urban youths who have turned to Christ because of these ministries. But honesty would lead urban youth workers to tell you that working among teenagers from the urban underclass requires that they learn to live with discouragement and disappointment.

One of the reasons for such failures is that cities are hard places to serve. The impersonality, anomie, and alienation that pervade the urban youth scene are of such dimensions that we find ourselves a bit overwhelmed. It is in the cities that the most horrible expressions of structural evil are found. It is in the cities that the allurements that are likely to seduce teenagers into destructive lifestyles are most prevalent. And it is in the cities that secularity has expressed itself in its most subtlely effective ways.

When I look at the socially disadvantaged communities where Nelson Copeland has served Christ over the past six years, I can easily see why it has been so hard for Christian youth workers to do the work of the Kingdom there. The schools become "blackboard jungles" where good education seldom occurs. Only 30 percent of those who enter West Philadelphia High School can be expected to graduate. And, of those who do graduate, more than half will do so as functional illiterates.

In the low-cost housing projects where Nelson has done youth ministry, almost half of all teenage males will have committed a major felony by the age of 18, and more than 50 percent of the female teenagers will have become pregnant by that age. The communities of the urban working poor are not easy places to minister.

But there is another reason why we have failed to relate the Gospel effectively to urban teenagers. It is because we do not grasp their cultural values and their basic orientation to life. We think they are Americans—just like the rest of us. But we are wrong. They are Americans—but they are *not* like the rest of us: They are culturally different.

Culture is a funny thing. It is hard for an outsider to grasp. Anthropologists seriously doubt that those who are raised outside of a given culture can ever really be at home in that culture. There are subtleties of language. There are differentiations of morality. There is a different world view (or weltanschauung, as the philosophers might say).

But the fact that the urban underclass is a culture that is alien to us middle-class youth workers who attempt to serve Christ in the midst of it must not prevent us from trying. When Jesus told us to go into *all* the world to preach the Gospel, he by no means excluded the urban underclass culture from the realm of that commission.

We must serve urban teenagers not only because God commanded us to do so, but also because there are so many of them. The proportion of the teenage population who are from disadvantaged urban communities is constantly growing. Hispanic-American youths, African-American youths, and Asian-American youths are more and more the wave of the future. They are where the action is, and most of them are living below the poverty level.

Nelson Copeland has provided us here with one of the first tools available. If we are to do the job that needs to be done, we need the techniques that go with cross-cultural communication, and Nelson has given us something to work with in this book. He is an African-American; and although he is not from the underclass, he has learned much from his six years of ministry in the city of Philadelphia.

In this book, he teaches us games that kids on the streets taught him. He is not as much a creator of games as a translator who helps us understand the messages of underclass teenagers. Through Nelson we can hear from the young people he has faithfully served, and from him we can learn some of the games that they really enjoy.

May he inspire you as he has inspired staff members of the Evangelical Association for the Promotion of Education to attempt a ministry in one of the most neglected mission fields in the world—urban America.

Tony Campolo
President of the Evangelical Association for the Promotion of Education

ACKNOWLEDGMENTS

• Special thanks to both Robin Littlejohn and Linda Jo Wychers—my major and minor proofreaders. Also to Noel Becchetti, of Youth Specialties, who helped tighten the text. Without you awl mye senttences wood knot bee good!

• The Evangelical Association for the Promotion of Education (EAPE). For six years we've grown together. You are always on my mind. Thanks for allowing me such free rein to lead your programs and to use your computer in the composition of this book.

•The Philadelphia Urban Youth Games Committee. The following are teenage friends of mine who served as a subcommittee to create and test many of these games: Douglas Ames, Toya Brown, Steven Davis, Dorinda Hampton, Calvin Jones, Eric Lawrence, Lupe Martin, Kenyatta Nobles, Charmaine Parrish, Harry Spenser, Jarmine Westmoreland, and Steven Williams.

• The following are brothers and sisters in urban youth ministry who chose to submit greatly needed activities: Matthew Bayley, Becky Cornwell, Michael Freeman, Judy Landis, Michael Moffit, Cindy Moon, Bill Mork, Andrew Nolan, Kamal Perkins, Jay Rosen, Donald Snavely, Julie Kring Schreifels, and Mindy Staley. To you, I extend my thanks.

• *HEY! YOU . . . LOOK!* If you have great, wonderful, creative games and activities that work with your city kids, send them to the following address: Reverend Nelson E. Copeland, Jr., 1906 Chelsea Road, Baltimore, MD 21216. If we receive enough suggestions for new games, your name will appear in the credits of the *next City Games* book.

• The games submitted as contributions are acknowledged as follows:

Douglas Ames—Kneel Dodge, Make It or Fake It, Blind and Seek, Lunch Date, Every Little Step I Take
Matthew Bayley—Top Gun
Toya Brown—Push-up Challenge
Becky Cornwell—ABC Scavenger Hunt, For Shapes Only, Flash Sentence
Steven Davis—Find That Tune, Puzzle Play, Day Lockup, Hit and Run, Tug Challenge, Fill the Bucket, Drug Deal, The Riddle
Michael Freeman—Jail Flag
Calvin Jones—Old Mule Race
Frank Kennedy—"Why"athelon
Judy Landis—Dinner Date, Scattergories, Feud It Out, For Close Friends Only, The Overground Times
Eric Lawrence—Color Me Quick, You Thief!
Lupe Martin—Snow Steps
Michael Moffit—First Aid Relay
Cindy Moon—Tickle Monster
Bill Mork—Phonics Game
Kenyatta Nobles—Egg in Mouth Relay, Shoot the Cream, Rhythm Youth Group, Put the Coin in the Funnel
Andy Nolan—Garden Planting
Kamal Perkins—Paint the Leaders
Philadelphia Urban Youth Games Committee—Dumb School, Squeeze the Lemon, Anna Banana, O'Clock
Jay Rosen—Beach Ball Blitz
Donald Snavely—Tour de Neighborhood
Julie Kring Schreifels—My Hero, Make Your Own Billboard, Environmental Mural, Planting in Faith, All Saints Day, What Would God or the Devil Say?
Harry Spenser—Manhunt, Roof Leap
Mindy Staley—Guess-o, Color-o
Jarmine Westmoreland—Dance Till You Drop

The Secret of Urban Play

Creating and executing successful games and activities for city kids can often be a great pleasure; at other times, urban games can become very difficult and nerve-racking. This phenomenon has faced many youth ministry organizations and has raised some formidable questions among urban youth ministers.

- "Why is it that the same game I used yesterday is a complete flop today?"
- "We did so much planning, I knew we had a hit. We started with lots of kids. So why are we now struggling to keep the ones we have?"
- "Why are there less resources available for us in urban youth ministry?"
- "All of my activities are old. Fresh ideas just don't exist for me anymore. Are there any creative things I can do when I'm completely dry?"

Urban youth ministers have to offer a different approach than is now being used. As I visit and meet representatives of different urban youth ministry organizations from around this country, my most common observation is that many of these ministries are trying to entertain the youths of *urban* America using the techniques of *suburban* America. The city requires its own characteristic techniques, unique to itself. It is up to the workers in urban ministry to begin to take hold of this profession and create games and activities that arise from the soil of the urban ministry itself. This book is an initial step in that direction.

Games that relate most effectively to city kids tend to be those activities that have an "urbocentric" core. Urbocentric games are an active attempt to consider the contemporary culture, the social characteristics, and the religious understandings of today's urban youth culture.

CULTURAL CONSIDERATION

There have been many discussions about whether or not culture plays a significant role in preparing and executing successful games for urban youths. It has been my experience that it does. Every cultural group has within itself the internal secret of what entertains those kids best. For example, if you were to take a culturally diverse segment of teens, break them into groups by race, and then ask them to put to music a phrase of poetry you hand out, you will find that each group tends to create a song that has traits characteristic of the music style and form of that group's culture (see Chapter 12 for this game).

Culture must be considered. It is the pulse by which urban youths live. When you consciously consider the culture of your kids, you will have more than a game—you will have found and expressed the exciting core of who they are. We must take note of this, or we will fail because we are creating games in our image instead of in theirs.

In Minneapolis, I had a discussion with a man who insisted culture did not need to be considered in order for a game to be successful with urban teens. "Relationships are all that matter," he stated. "I can do any game I want and my kids will love it." What this gentleman has misunderstood is that all games are based on culture. This European-American man working with African-American youths did not understand the implications of his statement. I was not arguing whether or not the kids were enjoying his activities—kids love anything that is exciting. I wanted him to realize that his method of gaming was not the kind that youth workers of African-American descent would normally identify with. Essentially he was creating and implementing games out of his cultural background instead of out of the cultural background of the youths. In short, the kids were enjoying being like him, instead of like themselves.

SOCIAL CONSIDERATION

The second consideration when creating urbocentric games is the social lifestyle of city youths. The games people play can tell us much about their interests and their socioeconomic status, because they are a reflection of social class. For example, the upper classes favor golf and tennis. Those in the middle class gravitate toward bowling, baseball, football, and hunting. Working-class people tend to enjoy boxing, TV wrestling, and basketball. When playing games with urban youths, this must be considered. Why do the rich attend the opera and the poor a street show? Why do different economic classes play different games? The answer is simple—resources. Resources are available in decreasing proportion from upper to lower classes. It is not a lack of interest that keeps lower and underclass teens (who live predominantly in cities) away from golf or tennis; golf clubs and tennis rackets are beyond their resources. Wrestling, boxing, and basketball, on the other hand, are popular because they require no resources. Urban youth games, if they are to be urbocentric, must consider the social situations and backgrounds from which city kids come.

I direct programs with both urban and suburban African-American youths. One of the earliest lessons I learned was that although the kids are of the same race, their social situations sometimes leave them miles apart. Each group's social demands are different. When I ask the urban African-American kids what they want to do for fun, they usually suggest ideas that require few resources (football, tag, dodgeball, jump rope, a dance contest, or a rap/singing contest). When I ask the same question of suburban African-American kids, they usually suggest ideas that require many resources (a talent show or drama, skating, movies, a dance party, day trips to other cities, and youth conferences). Although these youths are culturally similar, they have different social and economic orientations that give them different viewpoints on many similar issues.

RELIGIOUS CONSIDERATION

The city is an amalgamation of religious influences. When planning activities for urban young people, understanding the religious backgrounds from which they come can be extremely helpful. Within any one community there can be many places of worship (mosques, synagogues, kingdom halls, temples, and Christian churches). For a young person, this is overwhelming. There are so many forms of religion that it is an incredible task to believe in Christianity.

I led a large senior high group that was extremely challenging because the youths fell into five belief categories: Christian, Black Muslim, Mormon, Jehovah's Witness, and agnostic. When pressed, all of them believed in a god—they just didn't know which one to follow. I often asked these youths, "Why do you come to this Christian youth group?" They consistently answered, ". . . Because Jesus is my Savior, too."

In urban America, Christ is proclaimed in many forms. To the Black Muslim, he is a great prophet. To the Mormon, he is a son of God. To the Jehovah's Witness, he is God's first begotten. The agnostics tend to believe in Jesus historically. In short, urban activities that communicate only "JESUS" are not enough. Games must be specifically defined, overtly evangelical in their messages, and they must proclaim that Jesus become *Lord* of the kids' lives.

ZEITGEIST CONSIDERATION

Zeitgeist is a German term meaning the total climate of an era—the spirit of the times. It also describes the influence of the present age on an individual. We must be aware of the changing spirit of urban youth culture. If urban youth workers don't keep up with what's "in," we might be planning an activity that's "out." It is of utmost urgency that youth ministers considering the culture and social situations of city adolescents and children, remember this: Urban youth culture evolves and changes; urban youth ministry must also evolve to remain effective.

There have been times when I planned an activity that flopped simply because I forgot to set it in the context of the city. For example, I was going to teach third and fourth graders how to appreciate African-American art, so I displayed photographs of paintings for the kids to view. I attempted to point out facial features, body spacing, and the importance of foreground and background. I asked them, "What do you think the painter is trying to show us in this picture?"

After a while, I realized that many kids did not care for this activity. When I asked them why, they stated, "It's stupid. You don't always 'see' stuff." After pressing the issue and not getting anywhere, I gave them an assignment for the following day. I wanted them to bring a record album from home that had some form of art on it. The next day, we viewed the albums and I asked what they believed the artists were trying to portray. As I had guessed, discussion took off immediately. They saw deep artistic meaning in the album covers because they knew the words of the songs on the albums and could descriptively express what the artists were trying to portray (see Chapter 12). In short, although the original activity had a cultural and social basis, it was missing a third important urbocentric facet—the zeitgeist. Zeitgeist is the glue that fuses cultural and social considerations making an activity relevant to today's city youths.

MAKING GAMES HAPPEN

Now let's go one step beyond urbocentricity to the specifics of how to execute urban games. The best executed urban games result from a fourfold philosophy, summarized with the acronym *S.E.R.V.*

First, the best urban games are spontaneous. Spontaneity is exciting. Many of us youth workers play games over and over until the original fun we had with the game is lost. Creating spontaneity involves the ability to organize, rework, and perform activities afresh, so that each time you participate in a recurring activity, it is as if it has never been played before.

One time I was getting ready to play a variation of dodgeball with a group of eighth and ninth graders. When the time came for me to perform this game, a tall, lanky, 14-year-old named Dion opened the door and came in. Like always, he had a basketball under his arm. He looked confused and mad about something. I said, "Dion! You're late. Come in and take a seat now!" He stared at me, unmoved, as if he was not going to do it. I proceeded, "If you're not going to sit, then I guess you will have to go home." He walked slowly to his seat, trying to anger me. Noticing I was unfazed by his antics, he took the basketball and threw it at me as hard as he could. I caught it in midair. By this time, every young person's eyes were riveted on me, wondering what my next move was going to be. My normal procedure would have been to ask him to leave, but I sensed the opportunity for something spontaneously creative. With my hand still stinging from the force of the throw, I looked to the young man seated directly across the circle from me and threw the ball to him. The group laughed. Soon the kids were tossing the ball around as fast and as hard as they could—to see if anyone would drop it. Believe it or not, this lasted for 20 minutes: What began as a tense moment ended as a game.

This is what makes activity delightful for kids. I call it "Pentecost fun." Pentecost fun is the ability to realize that although a game is planned, the game can never be enjoyed until "something" spontaneously falls upon the group—you can't explain it, but all you know is that you're having fun. Sometimes, however, spontaneity can be planned. You've heard the phrase, "I'm planning to have fun tonight." What does this imply? It is tacitly saying that this person has categorized her or his evening in such a way that it will be conducive to fun. The evening will become more and more spontaneous, but only because the red carpet was laid for it in advance. Urban youth workers need to plan for spontaneity in their activities, instead of just letting things happen. That way, if things get out of hand, you know when and where to pull the plug.

Second, the best urban games are existential (meaning they arise out of the life experiences of the kids). It is important that the message sent through a game is one that kids can decode. In order for a game to fully realize its potential, it must be understood by all the participants. In other words, a game, activity, or curriculum works best when it meets kids where they are. When you plan activities that complement the experiences of urban youths, they will be interested.

Games that are existential work best when explained within the group's frame of reference—that is, according to the perceptions the kids have of their world. Every member in a given group shares certain perceptions of the world with other members of that group. Urban young people are no different. We must accommodate their perceptions of the world into how we execute activities. This is extremely important. I once was sitting in on a youth group where an activity was failing terribly. In frustration the youth leader yelled, "What's wrong with ya'll?" They replied, "We don't understand what you mean by this game." The problem here was not the game, but how the game had been explained to the kids. The youth leader proceeded to explain the game again, but this time he used terminology and illustrations that the group understood. Once it was reexplained, someone in the group said, "Oh! Well, why didn't you say that the first time?" Good games are existential and should flow out of the experiences of urban young people, plus be explained with those experiences in mind.

Third, the best urban games are repetitive. Repetition is a key to any exercise that is meant for learning. Urban educators continually put emphasis on repetition as a tool for activities intended to teach kids. Chapters 7-13 of this book are specialized activities that have been created for learning purposes. Repetition is recommended for many of these activities.

There are two primary reasons why repetition is a successful teacher. First, to repeat is to remember. When you ask children to repeat a process, you are no longer the impetus for their instruction—they are. In order to repeat something properly, the individual must remember what she or he is repeating. As a child in Sunday school, I constantly repeated Scriptures, sang Scriptures, or played competition games using Scripture. Even if I didn't understand the Scripture, I was able to repeat it with accuracy.

The second reason repetition is successful among urban youths is because repetition breeds comprehension. Have you ever done an activity with kids that you felt was extremely important? They remember everything you teach—but only for the game's purpose. After the game is completed, they usually can't remember what they learned. This is where repetition for remembrance falls short, and repetition for comprehension takes over. "Comprehension" repetition involves the use of games and activities that are done so that the youths will not forget what they have learned (see "You Thief" in Chapter 8). Comprehensive activities tend to involve some form of repetitive action that is written or verbal or visual.

An example of a comprehensive activity was the month-long team teaching that we did with a group of junior high school youths on homelessness. We studied the facts and the stats, did repetitive activities, brought in spokespersons on the topic, and studied how we thought Jesus would handle this issue. After three weeks of this, it dawned on my team that the youths cognitively understood the issue, but they had no concern to do anything about it. Our solution was simple—feed the homeless. The following week we took the group to feed homeless persons. The response was amazing. The kids who one week before seemed extremely uninterested in this topic were making statements like, "Let's do this once a month," "Why doesn't the city do something about this?" "Matthew 25 is right: What you do for the least of these, you are doing for Jesus." This is the type of activity that breeds comprehension because it directly involves the participants with the issue.

Finally, the best urban games are visual. If you've ever observed any city, you know that people are bombarded with visual stimulation. It amazes me how many billboards there are in Philadelphia. On one residential street, I once counted 14 advertising signs and billboards. For young people growing up in urban America, there is really no need to investigate, to search, to find, or to think because the world has literally been laid out before their eyes.

Someone once asked me, "Why don't city kids like to read much?" I answered, "Why should they want to read? Reading is for those who want to learn cognitively. City kids learn visually." There are two ways to learn about something: we can read about it or we can see it. These both have equal importance, but the more I speak to urban educators, the more I think they have decreased their emphasis on teaching Johnny to read; they are teaching Johnny to visualize.

Learning by visualization can be a useful tool for creating an activity that young people will enjoy. Urban youths tend to remember in detail those things that can be seen or touched. It is not the purpose of this book to take sides about which method of teaching is correct. I have become convinced that for city kids the more visual an activity is, the better. Therefore, be demonstrative in the games and activities you intend for learning (see "Color-o" in Chapter 8).

In conclusion, the secret of urban play is to create exciting games that use limited resources in the context of an urban setting. This book is dedicated to the profession of urban youth ministry. May it be helpful to all who work in that great place called the city. And may it be a worthy contribution in a field of study that constantly needs new resources.

Mixers

CHAPTER 2

BAREFOOT SHOE SEARCH

RECOMMENDED GRADES:
8-12

The objective is simple—find your shoes. The first person to success-fully find them, tie them on, and get back to the leader wins. First, have the group form a circle. Second, all players must take their shoes off and place them (untied) in front of their feet. Next, the group rotates in a clockwise direction, continuing in that direction until the leader says, "Shoe search!" When this is heard, players rush to their own shoes, tie them on securely, and run to the leader. The first one there wins that round. This game works best with groups of 20 to 30.

MATERIALS NEEDED:
Shoes.

RECOMMENDED GRADES:
6-10

BEACH BALL BLITZ

MATERIALS NEEDED:
Chairs, beach ball.

If you want fun, here it is. This activity is a scramble game for a large group. All you need are chairs and a beach ball. First, form the chairs in a square, so in essence you have four teams. Once young people are seated, have them count off by fours. Explain to the group that a number will be called out, and those with that number must run into the middle and attempt to kick the beach ball over the heads of their teammates. The first person to kick a "field goal" wins his or her team a point. The first team to reach ten points wins. This is extremely funny to watch.

RECOMMENDED GRADES:
3-8

COOKIE SORT

MATERIALS NEEDED:
Assorted cookies.

This is a fun mixer that allows you to eat when finished. The larger the group, the better. To begin, distribute a cookie to each person. When the leader tells the group to begin mixing, the players begin to look for others with the same kind of cookie they are holding. Once the cookies are matched up, the kids sit down together and begin sharing some information about themselves with their group. The leader should determine these questions. Once all the groups have discussed the questions raised, end with the kids eating their cookies. The following questions are good to use:

1. If you and your mother were about to die of hunger and you had one cookie left, would you eat it?
2. What is your favorite cookie?
3. If the world decided not to make any more cookies by the year's end, what would you do?
4. Tell six things about yourself, each one beginning with one of the letters in the word *cookie*.

EIGHTY-FIVE

RECOMMENDED
GRADES:
3-8

**MATERIALS
NEEDED:**
None.

This is a rhythmic, clapping, quick-wit game that can eliminate many players quickly. To get underway, have the group sit in a circle so everyone can see each other. If your group is unfamiliar with each other, have the players introduce themselves. Choose a person to begin the game. The game is recited as follows:

Hands up (clap, clap)
To eighty-five (clap, clap)
Gonna get (clap, clap)
Names of (clap, clap)
[Name any subject or category; for example, dogs] (clap, clap)
Three piece [or any number to ten] (clap, clap)
And no release (clap, clap)
No hesitation (clap, clap)
No relation (clap, clap)
Starting with (clap, clap)
[Name someone] (clap, clap)

The rhythmic pattern continues as the person named calls out three kinds of dogs without losing beat. For example, pit bull (clap, clap), German shepherd (clap, clap), Labrador (clap, clap). If the beat is broken, the person is out. If the youth successfully names three kinds of dogs, he or she continues the song from the top.

FOUR CORNERS

RECOMMENDED
GRADES:
8-12

This outdoor mixer is to be executed at intersecting street corners. The intersection you choose should not be heavily traveled by moving vehicles; a residential side street will do. If possible, have a youth

MATERIALS NEEDED:
Index cards,
street corners.

group sponsor on each of the corners. The ideal number for this activity is 16 to 24 people. First, on four cards write out questions (one per card) that can help kids find out information about each other (something about school, goals, or family, for example). Then count out enough cards so that each group member can receive one, and write on the cards different combinations of the numbers one to four. These cards tell the order in which the youths go to each of the four street corners at the intersection. When the group is ready to play, assign a number to each corner of the intersection and place a question card at each corner. Then give each youth one of the cards with the number combinations. When the leader says, "Go!" players walk directly to the street corner that corresponds with the first number on their cards. The group that gathers at each corner discusses the question it finds there. After a couple minutes, the leader calls for the kids to walk to the corner that corresponds to the second number on their cards, and so on.

RECOMMENDED GRADES:
7-12

GUESS THE SIGNATURE

MATERIALS NEEDED:
Index cards,
pencils.

The object of this game is to match the printed signature of the members of the group with their handwritten notes. It is a good way to begin to know names. This mixer works best with eight people. First, have everyone within the group write on index cards in cursive handwriting one sentence that is determined by the leader (for example, The rain in Spain falls mainly on the plain). Have the participants fold their cards and put them in a pile in the middle of the group.

Next, on another piece of paper, each individual must write his or her complete name. This time, however, the signature must be printed, not written. This is what makes the game difficult.

After this is done, one person at a time displays her or his printed signature to the group, allowing time for all to inspect it. The group then compares the signature with all the cursive sentences to determine a match. If group members make a correct match, the writer admits it; if they don't, play continues until a correct match is made. The process continues until the group has matched all the signatures with the sentences.

HERE I STAND

RECOMMENDED GRADES: 7-12

MATERIALS NEEDED: None.

This game requires a big group circled around the leader. Break the crowd into five smaller groups, each group gathering at a different spot in the circle. Tell the kids that this is an activity to see where people stand on controversial issues. Convince them to stick to what they believe and waver for nothing. Then ask, "Do you believe it is a Christian's responsibility to remain sexually pure?" Have the groups discuss this for five minutes. Then tell each group to say, "Outta here!" to one or two people who didn't conform to the group's consensus. The rejected ones move clockwise into another group. Then raise issue two: "Should women be allowed to have abortions?" Repeat the process. Do the same thing for issue three: "Why do some races seem to have more money and opportunities than others?"

Once all of this has been completed, ask those who were rejected from certain groups to tell why they think they were rejected. Begin an open discussion on the consequences of convictions. Shape the conversation to bring the young people to acknowledge that their beliefs can affect how they are accepted by certain groups. Then challenge them to consistently make decisions that would make Jesus rejoice.

JAR ME

RECOMMENDED GRADES: 7-12

This is a wonderful big group activity. Give every member a jar, paper, and a pencil. All players must write three things on the paper:

MATERIALS NEEDED:
Many jars, writing paper, pencils, timer.

their initials, three colors they have on, and the type of shoes they are wearing. Once this is completed, have the players put their papers in their jars. Collect all the jars, display them on a table before the group, and scramble them around. On the leader's signal, each individual takes a jar, opens it, and attempts to find the person described in the jar. Once that person is found, the pair must discuss the following information about themselves:

1. Name, age, and school attending
2. Three things the pair has in common
3. Each one describe his or her three favorite family members

What makes this game fun is that it is almost impossible to complete without some confusion. When you are looking for the person from your jar, someone is looking for you, and the person you are looking for is trying to find someone else! What gives this game its edge is that it will only last five minutes. That is, you will have to find and interview the person in your jar and be found and interviewed by the person who has you in his or her jar within that time limit. When the questioning is completed, players put the papers back in the jars and return them to the table. The process can now be repeated. This activity is excellent for a large group that has never met before.

RECOMMENDED GRADES:
9-12

KWANZAA MIX

MATERIALS NEEDED:
None.

Kwanzaa is an African-American holiday that celebrates the unity of the race (December 26-January 1). The term itself is Swahili for "first fruits." There are seven tenets to *Kwanzaa*. The relationship between these seven tenets should be understood by the leader. In brief, they are the following:

1. *Umoja* (racial unity)
2. *Kujichagulia* (self-determination)

3. *Ujima* (collective work and responsibility)
4. *Ujamaa* (cooperative economics)
5. *Nia* (racial purpose)
6. *Kuumba* (creativity)
7. *Imani* (faith)

This activity requires a group of 28 persons in four groups of seven. Within each group, each member of the group identifies himself or herself with one of the seven *Kwanzaa* principles. To begin, each group is given a scenario that pertains to an issue facing African-American people. The group makes up a solution to the problem by harmonizing each of the principles of *Kwanzaa*. Each group has no longer than ten minutes to find a solution to its problem scenario. Discuss each group's solution.

Below are a few scenario suggestions.

1. African-American males are missing in the nuclear family. Many say it is because they lack a sense of responsibility. Others say it is a result of social circumstances not in favor of the African-American male. How would the principles of *Kwanzaa* help people create a solution to this dilemma?
2. Teenage pregnancy among African-Americans is often a problem. Many female teens say, "I want a baby, someone I can love. What's wrong with wanting a child? I can take care of it, even if the father isn't around." How would the principles of *Kwanzaa* help people create a solution to this situation?
3. There has been debate over whether one should be called *black* or *African-American*. How would the principles of *Kwanzaa* help people create a solution to this issue?
4. Drugs and crime are rampant. Particularly among African-Americans, homicide is high. Many would say it is genocide. Many would say it cannot be solved. Will crime cause the destruction of the African-American community, or is there another solution? How would the principles of *Kwanzaa* help people create a solution to this issue?

Afterward, allow each group to exchange one or two of its members for one or two members of other groups. However, the exchange must be based on the principle a given member has chosen to represent. In other words, the teen from group one who is identifying with *Umoja* may only exchange places with an *Umoja* from another group. This activity allows creative discussion that really involves young people. It can be extremely informative culturally.

RECOMMENDED
GRADES:
1-4

MY SHIRT, YOUR NAME

**MATERIALS
NEEDED:**
Masking tape.

This game helps children to get to know each others' names. Begin by taping a line on the floor for the children to line up behind. Twelve feet ahead of the line, tape a circle large enough to enclose a portion of your group—this is the "huddle spot." Next, after explaining the rules, yell a shirt color you know some kids have on. The kids wearing this color run to the huddle spot and begin to ask for each others' names. When the group members think they can remember the names of everyone in their huddle, they return to the lines of children, and each member tells aloud the names of the rest of the kids from the huddle. Remember, this must be done within 45 seconds. To continue play, pick another color and repeat the process.

RECOMMENDED
GRADES:
6-12

PICKPOCKET

**MATERIALS
NEEDED:**
Random objects.

The object of this activity is to see how many people in the group can correctly choose which pant pocket a hidden item is in. To begin, pick a volunteer who has back pant pockets. Out of the group's sight, put one small item in each of the volunteer's back pockets. When this is done, the volunteer must stand with his or her back to the group in order that the back pockets may be seen. Next, the leader names one of the items in the pockets and ask the kids to decide which pocket holds that item and move to the side of the room the chosen pocket is near. Once everyone has moved to one side or the other, the items are shown to determine who guessed correctly. Those who guessed incorrectly must do one thing the winning group commands (for example, jumping on one foot, ten push-ups, spinning until dizzy). This game can be repeated many times.

PUZZLE PLAY

RECOMMENDED
GRADES:
5-12

**MATERIALS
NEEDED:**
4 complete
puzzles.

This activity is for a group of 16. To begin, set up four tables with a different complex puzzle scrambled on each table. Next, have everyone count off in fours. Have each number head to a different table. When the leader says, "Go!" each group has two minutes to piece together what it can of the puzzle. When the time is up, the twos and fours rotate clockwise, while the ones and threes rotate counterclockwise. This process of rotation gives each group a chance at each table. This activity can take a good while. Reward the first group to complete a puzzle.

QUESTION TOSS

RECOMMENDED
GRADES:
6-12

**MATERIALS
NEEDED:**
A shoe box,
writing paper,
pencils, tape.

For starters, have the young people sit in one big circle. Have them tear their papers in two and write two questions they would like others in the group to answer about themselves. Each half sheet should be folded and put in the shoe box. Tape the shoe box shut, but cut a door in its top for people to draw out questions. Now the toss begins! The person who has the box first tosses the box to anyone in the circle. That person takes out one question and answers it before the group (and then that question should be discarded). This is where the hilarity sets in. The game continues when the box is tossed to someone else.

This game can be a knockout, especially if you set the box up with a few gag questions. See to it the box is not constantly being tossed to the same people. Get everyone involved.

ROTATION EDUCATION

**MATERIALS
NEEDED:**
Chairs.

This mixer allows urban teens and children to educate an incoming staff of volunteers or interns. It can also help a large staff deal with issues by asking questions of a rotating group of youths.

First, the staff must be broken into four groups of three. Next, assign three kids to each group. The leader will raise issues that the teens will counsel the staff on. A few suggestions are as follows:

1. What are some steps to take to break up a fight?
2. What three characteristics do you look for most in a youth staff member you would share things about yourself with?
3. What makes a youth group boring for you? What would liven it up?
4. What things would you want someone who has never worked with city kids to know before he or she begins to work?

After the youths respond to the staff on the first issue, the staff can ask the kids questions about that topic. Give about ten minutes for dialogue on each issue. When the first topic has been discussed, the teens must rotate clockwise to another group. The leader can then announce another issue to be discussed. This should continue for four rotations.

SHARE SHUFFLE

RECOMMENDED GRADES:
6-12

This game is crazy. First, circle chairs into two rings facing each other; the outer ring faces inward, the inner ring faces outward. Inner and outer rings need the same number of chairs. Kids sitting in the outer ring shuffle clockwise, and kids sitting in the inner ring shuffle counterclockwise. When the leader yells, "Go!" each ring of kids must move in its given direction until the leader yells, "Stop!" Once stopped, the people facing each other must say their names and describe their favorite part of the city and why they like it. Other questions can be used. Only 30 seconds are given for the dialogue before the process continues. The larger the group, the more the fun.

MATERIALS NEEDED:
Many chairs.

SHARE THE DREAM

RECOMMENDED GRADES:
8-12

This game works best with 30 people who don't know each other well. First, ask the youths to visualize their futures and what they want to become. Next, have the kids mingle throughout the room attempting to form a group with kids who hold similar dreams for the future. When most kids are paired up or in groups, have everyone sit down. Draw the kids' attention to the different sized groups—some are large, some small, and some people might be alone. Have the teens notice that some dreams are popular, while others are unique.

Finally, allow time for the groups to discuss a plan of action to pursue these dreams. If someone is alone, encourage him or her to come up with a plan of action as well. Afterward, have each group share with the others its plan of action and discuss the joys or frustrations of its conclusions. End the discussion by saying that God has given all of us dreams to pursue. Some dreams will be easy to accomplish, and others will be difficult; but never give up on your dreams.

MATERIALS NEEDED:
None.

TALENT GUESS

**MATERIALS
NEEDED:**
Writing paper,
pencils.

Everyone has gifts and talents. This guessing game allows young people to guess the talents of their peers or face the consequences. To begin, on paper have young people write three talents they feel they have or three things they are good at. Afterward, have them fold their lists and put them in their pockets. Next, everyone must pair off, facing each other with person one's hands on person two's palms.

The objective is for person one to guess all three talents of person two in less than a minute. If person one guesses incorrectly, person two says, "Wrong" and tries to slap the hand of person one before it is moved. The guessing continues until the minute is up. Roles and hands switch, and person two becomes the guesser.

Once each of the pair has been the guesser, have the kids find new partners and continue the process using the same talent lists as before. This game can last for a good while. When it is over, knowing people better will compensate for sore hands.

TRY TO FIND ME MIXER

**MATERIALS
NEEDED:**
Writing paper,
trash bags,
pencils, apple.

This is an outdoor activity to mix teens up—literally. It mixes youths all around their neighborhoods. You must have two groups of six. Each person is given three pieces of paper and three trash bags. Piece one says *names*; piece two says *objects*; piece three says *mix*. The goal is to see which team can go out into the neighborhood and get the most information in each category within 40 minutes.

In the first category, team members must get as many signatures as they can. In the second category, they need to collect and record as many objects as they can (be sure to tell kids to pick up objects that are not dangerous). The objects in the bag must be recorded or they will not count. Each entry in the first two categories will be worth 1,000 points. However, in the third category, the team must find a member of the other team to get its final instruction. These instructions must be kept in sealed envelopes. If the other team members open the envelope, their team loses 10,000 points.

The final instruction should be a map to some prize that is strategically placed far away from the starting point. The map should require the team members to use mathematical skills, find someone with a password, get an address, make a phone call, or visit someone. There is only one prize, but it's only worth 3,000 points. In short, it is more beneficial to do parts one and two than it is to go after the prize. Consequently, the prize box should hold an apple and a slip of paper stating that the finder needs to get at least four signatures from the opposing team before time runs out, or the 3,000 points won't count. By this time, the kids hate this prize.

When the time is up, the teams returning late lose 500 points per minute. The winning team gets a real prize. This game is hilarious to watch.

VEHICLE MIX

This activity is great on a bus or van trip. When you reach a prolonged stoplight, yell, "Switch." The children have ten seconds to switch seats in the vehicle while you count down. After doing this at two or three lights, the kids will definitely be awake. CAUTION: Be sure the vehicle remains stopped until all the children are reseated.

WANNA BANNA ZOOM

This game is a great way to get kids to introduce themselves in a big group. First, set up chairs in a circle, facing inward. There should be

MATERIALS NEEDED:
Chairs.

one less chair than there are people, and there should be spaces between them. Have everyone stand behind the chairs. The game begins when the leader slowly says the game title, "Wanna . . . Banna . . ." while everyone rotates around the chairs in a clockwise direction. When the leader gets to the word *Zoom!* each person rushes for a chair. The person who is not fortunate enough to get a chair has to answer two general questions from the group. Once the questions are answered, the process can be repeated. The following questions are good to use:

1. Why did you come tonight?
2. Which of your family members are you the most like?
3. If you were stranded on an island and had to choose one person from this room to live with, who would it be?
4. Describe yourself in three words.

RECOMMENDED GRADES: 5-12

WHO-A YOU-A ME-A

MATERIALS NEEDED:
None.

This game allows the kids to introduce themselves in a funny way. Everyone should be seated or standing in a circle. Choose someone in the circle to begin the introductions, which are continued in a clockwise direction as follows:

Person one: Who-a
Person two: You-a
Person one: Me-a (giving name) Nelson-a
Person two: (Turns to person three) Who-a
Person three: You-a
Person two: Me-a Renee-a
Person three: (Turns to person four) Who-a
Person four: You-a
Person three: Me-a Dave-a

Continue this process until all the players have introduced themselves. This can become extremely hilarious, especially because many urban youths have nicknames: Mookie-a, Rambo-a, Ne-Ne-a, Pooh-Pooh-a (to name just a few).

"WHO"DLUM

RECOMMENDED GRADES: **4-10**

MATERIALS NEEDED:
Paper.

This is a terrific guessing game for 20. To start, the group must sit in a circle. Hand out folded slips of blank paper to everyone. One slip of paper has the word *hoodlum* printed on it. The person who receives this slip must be secretive. In a clockwise direction, each individual must take a guess at who the "hoodlum" is. Each individual takes a guess (of course the hoodlum chooses someone else) until it has been deduced who the hoodlum is. If the hoodlum is not found within four minutes, the game is over and this person is revealed.

WHO'S WHO

RECOMMENDED GRADES: **6-12**

MATERIALS NEEDED:
Writing paper, pencils, chairs.

This mixer is for a large group of people who are unfamiliar with each others' names. By the end of this mixer, you might not know everyone's name, but you will know quite a few. Start by writing down the names of all the kids playing the game. Have the group form two concentric circles with an equal number of chairs; the outer circle faces inward, and the inner circle faces outward. When the leader signals the game to begin, the outer circle moves in a clockwise direction, while the inner circle moves counterclockwise. Players say their own names over and over as they circle and, at the same time, attempt to remember the names that they hear. The circle should rotate four times. When everyone is finally seated and dizzy, quickly hand out paper and pencils so the players can record as many names as they can remember. Find out who has listed the most names correctly. End the game by asking all the participants to stand and introduce themselves formally.

RECOMMENDED
GRADES:
6-9

"YOU DON'T KNOW?"

**MATERIALS
NEEDED:**
None.

This game is a fun way to get to know about people. To begin, form a circle. When a directional flow for the game has been chosen, pick someone to begin the game. Person one asks person two, "You don't know?" Person two says, "Know what?" Person one goes on to ask any question of person two ("What's your name?" "Who's your favorite rap artist?"). Person two answers, then looks to person three and repeats the process by stating, "You don't know?" The game can last as long as the fun lasts.

RECOMMENDED
GRADES:
7-12

YOU'RE MY BABY

**MATERIALS
NEEDED:**
None.

In this dating game, the teens pick people who look like they would go well together. To start, ask for one volunteer. When that person has been identified, ask for three things he or she looks for in a potential date. Once this is known, have the person leave the room. The kids then decide who in the group seems to best fit those characteristics. Once this person is chosen, bring in the volunteer. Now the fun begins!

The volunteer looks the teens over and attempts to find the person the group chose for him or her. The volunteer approaches the person who he or she thinks the group chose and says, "You're my baby!" The group responds by shouting, "Yes!" or "No!" The volunteer receives three guesses only (depending on the size of the group). If he or she is successful, award a gag date or, if the couple is willing, a staff-chauffeured real date. If the volunteer fails to discover which person the group chose, the group reveals who it is.

Indoor Games for Small Groups

3

CHAPTER

CAR PINBALL

RECOMMENDED
GRADES:
K-4

Here's something for two kids to do on a car trip. On the floor of many cars, there is an elevated bump that divides the left and right sides of the car. This crazy game's objective is to see who can keep a tennis ball on the opponent's side the longest. To begin, place the tennis ball on the bump. Let the players know this game lasts one minute only. When the leader says, "Go!" each player struggles to keep the ball on the opponent's side using feet only. The one who has kept the ball on the other's side the longest wins. Proceed to another round. NOTE: As a precaution, be sure the players' doors are locked.

MATERIALS NEEDED:
Tennis ball, watch.

RECOMMENDED
GRADES:
8-12

CLUB BY PHONE

**MATERIALS
NEEDED:**
2- or 3-way
phones.

Here's an activity that can be done completely at home. Have a "Club by Phone." The recommended size is no more than ten young people. Parents must be notified of this activity since it ties up the phone for a while. The Club can be done as a conference call with the aid of an operator or the kids can use two-way or three-way phones or they can congregate at a house with multiple extensions. This enables many people to be heard on one line. Ironically, many urban youths live in homes with two or three extensions. It is the job of the youth director to orchestrate who should call whom so that the entire group of kids can be involved from their homes. Once this detail has been dealt with, the linkages should be established. Now you can begin the club. It should mimic the normal club structure of singing, prayer, discussion of an issue, and whatever else is unique to your club.

RECOMMENDED
GRADES:
K-3

COLOR ME QUICK

**MATERIALS
NEEDED:**
Chairs, crayons,
photocopies of
a coloring book
page.

This activity is ideal for a very small group. Make several photocopies of a page from a coloring book appropriate for your group's age. Set one of the pages and a box of crayons on each child's chair. Tell the players they must color an area of the picture at their chair until the leader says, "Time's up." Then they must rotate clockwise and start to color part of the picture sitting on another child's chair. The process continues in 15-second intervals until all pictures have been completed. Display the completed pictures to the group. This can lead into a discussion about teamwork or other related themes.

COUGH, SNIFF, SNEEZE

MATERIALS NEEDED:
None.

This is an imitation game where kids mimic the leader. It starts with the leader giving a single cough that the kids imitate. The leader proceeds to give different cough patterns—a fast cough, then a slow cough; loud, then silent coughing—and after each pattern, the kids copy the leader. Once the kids are with the activity, begin to sneeze, sniff, or mimic vocal sickness sounds. Then mix coughing with sneezing and sniffling. Really use your voice with this activity. Continue until the activity naturally expires, or you've gone hoarse.

CUP CLASH

MATERIALS NEEDED:
Cups, water, round table, chairs.

"Cup Clash" involves passing cups across a table to a partner without clashing with the cup stationed permanently in the middle. This is best done with a group of six. To begin, place a cup filled with water in the center of a large circular table. Pair up the young people and give one person in each pair a cup of water. The teammates must sit directly opposite each other at the table. The objective is to pass the cup back and forth to each other without hitting the cup in the middle. If for any reason your cup hits the middle cup, your team is eliminated (often, one team's cup pushes another's into the middle cup). The team lasting the longest wins the round. Since this activity is often completed in less than two minutes, it is best to have the winning team be the one that wins the best out of ten.

RECOMMENDED
GRADES:
7-12

ELEVATOR RACE

MATERIALS NEEDED: Elevator, stopwatches.

Most high-rise housing developments have elevators. The object of this game is to outrace an elevator. After obtaining permission from the building manager, divide the group into two even-numbered teams. One group will use only the elevator and the other only the stairs. This game works best with ten to 16 people.

Once the teams are chosen, each member picks a floor he or she will race to before racing back to the ground floor. Sponsors will be stationed on both the ground floor and on the designated floor for that race with stopwatches to record the times. Once this is established and team members are in their respective places, the race can begin. Be sure to stress the need for courtesy to the tenants of the building during this game.

The hilarity of this race is provided when regular tenants use the "racing" elevator; it slows that team's time. In short, you send one rider up, but the elevator returns with many riders. Each team takes a turn at both the elevator and the stairs.

RECOMMENDED
GRADES:
8-12

FEUD IT OUT

MATERIALS NEEDED: A bed sheet, blackboard, chalk.

This game is similar to the television show *Family Feud* except it involves four teams. At the session before the game is to be played, everyone must write out responses to seven pregame questions. These responses will be compiled to determine the top five answers.

Make up four teams of four people each. Each team gives itself a name. Next, one person from each team comes forward and raises his or her left hand. One of the survey questions is posed to them. The first one to slap a leg with her or his hand gets to answer. If the answer this person gives is among the responses compiled earlier, that person's team takes control. The team attempts to guess the rest of the veiled answers within one minute. If successful, the team receives 100 points; if unsuccessful, the other teams get one guess each. If their answers appear among the compiled responses, the teams that guess correctly split the points. If no one answers correctly, no one wins the round. Erase the blackboard and write out a new set of veiled answers. The team that wins the best out of seven rounds wins the game.

FIND THAT TUNE

RECOMMENDED GRADES:
5-12

MATERIALS NEEDED:
Blindfold, radio, large room.

One volunteer is blindfolded, and a second volunteer carries a radio tuned to a favorite station. The remaining group members are spectators for that round of the game and should remain quiet. Be sure the room is clear of all barriers and obstacles. To begin, place the blindfolded person and the radio person on opposite sides of the room. The objective is to time how long it takes the blindfolded person to touch the person with the radio. The catch is that the person with the radio can walk around (not dart or run). When one pair has finished, record its time and continue with another pair. There will be two winners: the blindfolded person with the shortest time, and the radio person with the longest time.

FOR CLOSE FRIENDS ONLY

RECOMMENDED GRADES:
9-12

MATERIALS NEEDED:
Paper, pencils.

Pair everyone with a partner of the opposite sex, then send the males out of the room. The emcee asks the ladies four questions about their partners. The following questions are examples: What will your partner do when he graduates high school? What's your partner's favorite ice cream? Who is your partner's favorite rap star? The ladies must respond in the manner they believe their partners will respond. Each answer they give should be written down on a separate sheet of paper that is then folded in half and placed on their laps, in order.

Once the ladies finish answering the questions, ask the males to return. The emcee then asks each male what he believes his partner's response to each question was. After the young man responds, his partner holds up her answer to see if the responses match. If they match, a point is given.

For round two, the females go out and the males answer questions. The couple who answers the most questions correctly wins a prize, or the staff could offer to take the couple out on a date.

RECOMMENDED GRADES:
9-12

HAIR SCARE

MATERIALS NEEDED:
Hair clippers, 2 chairs.

This is a challenge for those who are daring and for those who want to try their hands at barbering. There are four volunteers needed; two will cut and two will be clipped. Those who are to be clipped must give specific instructions to the "barbers." The instructions are to be given once. The barbers have ten minutes to complete the haircut. The group votes for the one who did the best job. That barber wins the title "Hair Scare Champion." If anyone's hair was butchered as a result, pay for the person to receive a professional haircut.

RECOMMENDED GRADES:
8-12

HIGH CHAIR

MATERIALS NEEDED:
Chairs.

This activity determines who can jump into the seat of the highest stack of chairs. For starters, push a four-chair stack against a wall. One by one, challengers run up to the chairs, jump, and land on the top seat. Those who clear this height receive an added chair on their next jump until a "High Chair" winner is chosen. CAUTION: Have two staff members stand on either side of the chairs to keep the chairs from falling over and to keep the challengers from hurting themselves.

LAUNDRY FOLDING CONTEST

This game involves individual effort. Set out several piles of clothes, and be sure each pile has the same number of garments. The object of this game is for each player to fold as quickly as possible the pile of clothes before him or her, load the laundry basket, carry the basket to the marker (15 feet ahead), and unload the basket. Make the piles big so it takes a couple of trips. The first person to have the items folded and unloaded at the marker wins. Stress that the clothes must be fully folded.

MATERIALS NEEDED:
Lots of clothes, laundry baskets.

MAKE ME SPLASH

This game allows you to have a spitting good time. To begin, mark the mug with a line and fill it up to the line with water. Ask for a volunteer who believes no one can make her or him laugh. Once selected, this person should fill his or her mouth with water until his or her cheeks bulge, and then hold the water in the mouth without swallowing any. If needed, add more water and change the water-level mark on the cup. The object of this game is to see who can hold the water in her or his mouth for 20 seconds without laughing or letting any of the water leak out. If any water leaks or the person laughs, he or she will be out. To be sure no one swallows any water and, therefore, cheats, the person who has successfully held his or her laughter for 20 seconds must spit the water back into the cup to see if the water meets the premarked level. If the water is below the mark, the person is disqualified. It's hilarious to view the young people painstakingly attempt to hold in the water. Many will not be so successful. The game can continue with a new volunteer and a fresh cup of water.

MATERIALS NEEDED:
Mug, water.

MISSING LETTER

**MATERIALS
NEEDED:**
None.

This activity can be used to focus kids' attention. Its purpose is to have a child pronounce a word you give that has a letter missing. This game can be played in one of two ways: Kids can pronounce their names or a word that is given.

For example, let's say we are playing by using the children's names. The leader will say, "Who can tell me what your first name is once the first letter is missing?" If the child's name is Christopher, the response will be Hristopher. You can change which letter or letters you leave out. This activity has worked exceptionally well in getting city kids to focus on what you want pronounced.

PAINT THE LEADERS

**MATERIALS
NEEDED:**
Water color
paint, brushes.

The leaders of the group dress up in light-colored clothing that paint will show up on. It is best if all their clothing can be painted (shoes and socks included). When the kids arrive, tell them they can paint you. Have them paint your clothing completely. Once the paint has dried, display this wonderful artwork for all to see.

PATTY FAKE

**MATERIALS
NEEDED:**
None.

This activity follows the same format and song as "Patty Cake." First, divide the group into pairs. One person becomes the "withdrawer," the other the "challenger." Both players begin to chant the "Patty Cake" rhyme and do the motions. Any time after they've gotten past the opening line "Patty cake, patty cake," the withdrawer may attempt to fake the challenger by withholding his or her hand. It is the challenger's responsibility to try to hit the hand anyway. Whoever wins two out of three rounds is decreed the better skilled player. Have the players switch roles and continue.

PIN THE TAIL ON THE YOUTH WORKER

RECOMMENDED
GRADES:
K-4

This activity follows the same rules as "Pin the Tail on the Donkey." The difference is the youth worker is the donkey! Kids love it. Cut out a cardboard tail. Use either velcro or tape to pin the tail to the human donkey.

MATERIALS NEEDED: Cardboard, velcro or tape, blindfold.

PUT THE COIN IN THE FUNNEL

RECOMMENDED
GRADES:
3-9

This game requires teams of two. One person from each team sits on the floor with a funnel held between her or his legs, the funnel tip touching the ground. The second person stands above his or her teammate with ten coins. Now the game begins. Person two places the coins one by one on person one's head. Person one attempts to flick the coin from her or his head into the funnel. The first team to successfully drop all the coins in the funnel wins. This activity is more difficult than it seems.

MATERIALS NEEDED: Coins, funnels.

READY, SET, BOUNCE

RECOMMENDED
GRADES:
K-4

The purpose of this activity is to determine who is the quickest to stand and sit when the leader gives the signal. To begin this game, the leader says, "Ready . . . Set . . . BOUNCE!" When the last word is said, the children leap up, then down. The first one down is acknowledged as the round winner. If any kids jump out of their seats early

MATERIALS NEEDED: Chairs.

49

(in anticipation of your words), they are out. This is a great activity for groups of eight or more.

RECOMMENDED
GRADES:
All

RHYTHM YOUTH GROUP

MATERIALS NEEDED:
None.

To begin this easy, rhythmic activity, form a circle. Using his or her mouth, hands, chest, or feet, one person starts and continues a single beat. In succession, each member in the circle adds a different beat that complements the original beat. Each player continues his or her beat throughout the game. No instruments are necessary.

RECOMMENDED
GRADES:
3-7

RUSH THAT NAME

MATERIALS NEEDED:
None.

To begin this game, the leader calls out a child's name. That child must respond by calling another child's name in less than two seconds. If someone takes too long to call out a name, everyone yells, "Rush that name" and tickles him or her. The leader puts the pressure on by counting the seconds out loud. The objective is to see how many kids can go until someone falters. Set a goal and see if you can reach it. The more the better for this activity, especially if the children are familiar with each other.

RECOMMENDED
GRADES:
6-12

SCATTERGORIES

MATERIALS NEEDED:
4 sheets of newsprint, markers, paper, pencils.

The purpose of this game is to have the teens use their heads to list items in a particular category. Post the four sheets of newsprint before the group. Each sheet is labeled with a category of the leader's choosing (for example, names of state capitals, boys' names, consumer products, movie titles, things that are cold). Next, a sheet of paper and a pencil are given to each youth. Players must list one to ten down their pages. The youth leader then chooses a letter of the alphabet for the first category and allows two minutes for each youth to list ten things in that category that begin with that letter.

For example, assume the category is consumer products, and the letter that was given is "P." The kids must list within two minutes as many consumer products as they can that begin with the letter "P." The list might consist of such products as peanut butter, pickles, paprika, or Post Raisin Bran. Each item listed is potentially worth one point. Consumer products listed that have more than one "P" in the name are potentially worth one point per word that begins with "P" (for example, *Peter Pan Peanut Butter* is worth three points).

When time is up, everyone tells what she or he wrote while the leader writes the items on the newsprint sheet. For every item that is listed by only one player, that player receives a point. Duplicate items will not receive points. Only items no one else has listed count for points. When scoring is completed, another category and letter can be chosen. This game can have as many rounds as desired.

SPY EYE

RECOMMENDED GRADES: 6-9

MATERIALS NEEDED: None.

If you want to talk about a game that can keep a person guessing, this is it. To initiate this game, have the group sit in a circle. Next, someone must be chosen to be "It." This person must then leave the room. The youth director explains to those remaining that this is a guessing game where "It" has to determine who the elected leader is. The group then chooses a leader, and this is what he or she must do. The chosen leader signals the group to slide from chair to chair to the left or the right by using her or his legs. If the leader moves his or her right leg, the group will move to the right. If the left leg is moved, the group will move to the left. If in the process of moving the leader sticks out her or his tongue, the group stops. The leader's actions are to be done secretly when the leader thinks she or he can signal the group without "It" noticing the actions. When the group understands the rules, "It" returns to stand in the middle of the circle until he or she guesses who the leader is. If the guess is correct, a new "It" is chosen; if incorrect, the game continues.

RECOMMENDED
GRADES:
5-8

TOP GUN

MATERIALS NEEDED:
Paper, chairs.

This is a paper plane relay. First, split the group into two teams. Give each team a piece of paper, and have the kids construct a paper plane they think will fly well. Next, have the teams form two lines. One member from each team is holding the paper plane while sitting in a chair ten feet in front of his or her team line. At the leader's permission to start, the person seated attempts to throw the plane to the front person on his or her team. It must land within reach or the seated person must get up and try again. If it is caught or lands within the team member's reach, the seated person runs to the end of the line while the person who caught the paper plane takes the seated position and continues the process. The first team to complete one rotation wins.

RECOMMENDED
GRADES:
3-9

TURKEY STARE

MATERIALS NEEDED:
None.

This is a stare game that seeks to determine who can look eye-to-eye with an opponent the longest, without laughing. The one who laughs first is a turkey. To proceed, ask two volunteers to come forward and stand with their backs to each other. When the leader gives them permission to begin, they immediately turn to each other and stare eye-to-eye. The first one to laugh or uncontrollably smile is the turkey. Avoiding eye contact gets a player only one warning before that person is the turkey whether he or she smiled or not. The winner is then challenged by another to determine if anyone can dethrone him or her.

THE WANDERER

RECOMMENDED GRADES:
K-4

MATERIALS NEEDED:
None.

The object of this game is for everyone to not only follow the leader ("The Wanderer"), but to act out the motions indicated by the story he or she is telling. Begin with everyone standing in a circle including the wanderer. The wanderer then proceeds to tell a story about his or her wanderings. As the story continues, the wanderer begins to walk and invites all the others to wander with him or her. The circle begins to follow. The wanderer's story can then take off anywhere and include actions like singing, running, galloping, lying down, jumping—anything. However, the most important point is for the wanderer to tell the story in such a way that the word describing the next action he or she will do comes immediately before that movement is made. The kids begin to anticipate what the next movement might be, and announcing it at the last minute catches kids off guard and sometimes leaves them shuffling into the wrong move.

WET BACK

RECOMMENDED GRADES:
6-12

MATERIALS NEEDED:
Plastic cup, water.

The object of this activity is to avoid getting wet by being still and not laughing. Play this game on a floor that can be mopped up easily. To begin, choose a volunteer who has the reputation of being very funny. Then have the players lay on their stomachs. As they are doing this, give a plastic cup full of water to the volunteer. Tell the group the volunteer is going to be placing the cup of water on the back of any individual he or she thinks can be made to laugh. The volunteer then places the cup on a secure area of the back of one player and tries for 15 seconds to make that person laugh so hard that the cup of water spills. If the volunteer is successful, the person with the wet back takes the volunteer's place and continues the game by placing a full cup of water on another player's back and trying to make him or her laugh. Once someone has a wet back, she or he cannot reenter the game as a player. The game continues until one player remains.

RECOMMENDED GRADES:
6-12

WHAT'S IT TO YOU?

MATERIALS NEEDED:
Table, chairs, coin piece, random objects.

The object of this game is to choose a dollar amount closest to the actual purchase price of an item. Two opponents sit at a table facing each other with an object on the table between them. A coin flip determines who bids first. The first bidder tells what he or she thinks the item costs. Then the second bidder estimates the cost. Each person gives three bids in alternating succession. However, if someone thinks his or her bid is extremely accurate, he or she can stop bidding at the first or second bid. The strategic advantage of stopping the bid is the opponent will also have to cease bidding. To stop, the person who is bidding says, "Stop this bid." The leader then reveals whose bid was the closest to the price of the item. That bidder wins. You can repeat many times with different objects.

RECOMMENDED GRADES:
2-5

WHITE OUT PAINTINGS

MATERIALS NEEDED:
Bottles of correction fluid, sketching paper.

The objective is to produce a painting. Instead of using paint or crayons, however, use correction fluid, which comes in many colors. Give your group the same picture to paint. Display the paintings when done.

Indoor Games for Large Groups

4 CHAPTER

ADVANTAGE

Here's a fun one for a big, diverse group. The challenge is for a younger kid to push an older one out of marked zone lines. The advantage is the younger kid can use his or her hands, while the older one cannot. The winner takes on another challenger. A taped zone box is needed; it must be 12 feet square. This activity can last for a while and can be fun, if the pushing does not get too rough.

MATERIALS NEEDED:
Masking tape.

BACK TO NOISE

This is a funny game that allows kids to focus up front and is best used with a group that needs to get rid of some energy. Begin by turning your back to the group. Tell the kids they must make as

MATERIALS NEEDED:
None.

much noise as possible until you turn to look at them. When you look around at the kids, they must cease all noise instantly. If anyone is caught, he or she is out and will now help you spot people still making noise when you turn around next time.

RECOMMENDED
GRADES:
3-7

BERLIN WALL

MATERIALS
NEEDED:
None.

To start this game, everyone must form a circle. After the circle is formed, select eight to 12 people (depending upon your total number) to stand in the middle of the circle and link arms, forming a wall. Once the wall team is in place, explain that its objective is to keep the others from breaking through. The leader then instructs those in the circle that they have ten seconds after their names are called to attempt to get through the wall.

RECOMMENDED
GRADES:
7-12

BLIND AND SEEK

MATERIALS
NEEDED:
Blindfolds.

Divide your entire group into two even-numbered teams. Have the two teams line up facing each other with a distance of six feet between them. Have each player remember the name of the person standing directly in front of her or him, since this person will be his or her partner. Once this is done, give a blindfold to every member. When blindfolds are on everyone securely, have two staff members switch those who are blindfolded around, to make the game difficult. When the leader gives the go, everyone calls the name of his or her partner, trying to find the partner as quickly as possible. When partners find one another, they sit and take off their blindfolds. This activity looks crazy in operation. The funniest part is watching some take off the blindfolds to find they are sitting with the wrong person! Great for groups that are unfamiliar with each other.

BOOKIE

RECOMMENDED
GRADES:
6-12

This game resembles the lifestyle of a "Bookie." Its purpose is to see who can remember the most information. To begin, ask for a volunteer to be the "bookie." Play this up: Ask for someone who thinks he or she can remember a massive amount of information. Announce, "The person who remembers the most receives a prize." Next, the bookie goes around the room as people give him or her either one name or number to remember. When this is completed, have the bookie regurgitate as much information as possible. Reward the bookie who remembered the most information.

MATERIALS NEEDED:
None.

DARK HUNTER

RECOMMENDED
GRADES:
8-12

This activity is appropriate around Halloween and works best if done in a house or a church. Choose several objects and hide them in the game area before the game begins. To begin, tell the group that you have hidden certain objects in the dark room or rooms where they will play the game. (If there are any rooms that should not be entered, make them known before the game begins.) Ask for a volunteer willing to go into a dark place, armed with a flashlight, and find one of the objects in less than five minutes. Make sure the hunter understands that he or she cannot leave the room until the object is found or five minutes expire. Once you have your volunteer hunter, tell the rest of the teens that they are to hide in the dark game area and listen for you to shout, "Run, hunter, run!" which means the hunter has not returned with the item he or she is seeking within five minutes. When the hidden players hear this, they must dash from their hiding places and attempt to stop the hunter by scaring the person before he or she can leave. If the hunter hears you scream, "Run, hunter, run!" he or she must exit swiftly before the hidden players

MATERIALS NEEDED:
Flashlight, random objects.

attack. If the hunter retrieves the hidden object before the time expires, he or she receives a reward. Send the hunter to stand outdoors while everyone else hides. Now the game can begin.

The most interesting thing about this activity is that, while searching, the hunter usually finds many of those who are hiding. This initially scares the hunter out of his or her wits, but is advantageous if escape is needed because he or she now knows where people are hiding. This game can be played as long as there are items to retrieve and people willing to hide.

RECOMMENDED GRADES:
5-12

DARK SURPRISES

MATERIALS NEEDED:
Random objects.

This activity is to take place in the dark. When kids enter the room, have them sit in a circle. At this point, turn every light out. Players are to guess what object is put in their hands as it's passed to everyone in the circle. An object can be handled for only five seconds at a time. After it gets around to everyone, have people guess what it is. Turn on the lights to prove what the object is to the group. Use objects like peeled grapes, slime, or toys. Continue play for a while, until you are ready for the last object, which is meant to scare the group. Live spiders work best. However, the last object will not actually be given to the person because, before you put it in his or her hands, someone will turn on the lights. This will literally be a scream.

RECOMMENDED GRADES:
8-12

FACE IT

MATERIALS NEEDED:
Bowls, long table, messy items.

Problems that are avoided eventually have to be dealt with, so "Face It." This is a game of challenge. You need a long table with about six messy items displayed in bowls (for example, Jell-O, a watermelon, honey, salad dressing, powder, spaghetti sauce).

Next, choose three volunteers and tell them, "You will be asked four questions by the group. If you fail to answer them, the group will say, 'Face it,' and you must dip your face in the item the group chooses." This activity allows youths to understand that problems and questions avoided can make them look foolish in the end. To liven things up, have someone throw in a question that is not personal, but hard. For example, if two men were killed in an accident, where would they bury the survivors? Or better, what is the square root of 171? Afterward, this activity can lead into a discussion about facing problems.

FLOUR TUG

RECOMMENDED
GRADES:
5-12

**MATERIALS
NEEDED:**
Tug rope, flour,
rag, masking
tape.

This is a slippery tug-of-war game with a difference—flour. To begin, split the group into two teams. If your group is very large, form three teams and let the odd team play the winners. Next, pour flour on the floor and the tug rope. Tie a rag on the rope's center and use masking tape to mark the center of the floor. Since this activity is a slippery one, warn your participants that horseplay will be frowned upon. When two teams have an adequate grip on the rope, allow the game to begin. The team that pulls the opposing team's lead person over the tape mark wins. Sounds easy, but not so when you're contending with a slippery floor and rope. This is a fun and zany activity.

HIT AND RUN

RECOMMENDED
GRADES:
4-10

**MATERIALS
NEEDED:**
Towel.

First, ask ten people to form a 20-foot diameter circle. Place a towel in the middle of the circle. Next, ask a volunteer to stand within the circle and be the "tagger."

The game begins when the youth leader walks around the circle and taps someone. When this happens, it is the objective of the tagger to snatch up the rag in the middle of the circle and dart back to his or her original spot before being tagged by the person who was tapped. If the tagger successfully returns to his or her spot, then the second person becomes the tagger. If the tagger is unsuccessful, the process continues until he or she wins back a spot.

HUMAN NOISEMAKER

MATERIALS NEEDED:
None.

This game involves one volunteer remembering and repeating the noises made by the group. This game works best with a group of 15 to 25. Begin by soliciting a volunteer. When the leader says, "Go!" everyone will make a tonal noise simultaneously. The volunteer has two minutes to go around the circle listening to each person and repeating sequentially what each individual says. No more than two tones or sounds can be made by each individual. When the time is up, the volunteer must repeat as many sounds as can be remembered and point to the person who made the sound. Count the number of successes. Then have a challenger repeat the process to determine if he or she can improve the number. This activity can continue as long as there is someone who believes she or he can improve the former standing.

KEY DECISION

MATERIALS NEEDED:
Locks, keys, prizes.

The object of this game is for your team to possess as many keys as possible in order to have a better chance at opening the presented door or chain lock. This is a game of tough questions and tough decisions. First, form four teams of four. The remaining youths make up the audience, who cheer on decisions. Second, display 20 keys but only one lock. Third, tell each group it will receive a 15-second huddle to come up with the answer to a tough question. If the team answers correctly, it gets to choose a key and see if it opens the lock.

The team that opens the lock receives a special prize (that can be revealed before or after the lock is opened).

The game does not stop here, however. The winning team now has an option to win a bigger prize, if it is willing to risk its present winnings. If the team accepts this round, three locks are brought out, but only one key. In order to obtain the key, team members must answer one more question. If they answer correctly, they are given the key and have one chance to choose the lock the key will open. If the key opens the lock they chose, they get both their winnings; if they are unsuccessful, they win nothing. This game can be repeated by choosing other teams from the audience and using different locks.

KNEEL DODGE

RECOMMENDED GRADES:
4-8

MATERIALS NEEDED:
Dodgeball or playground ball.

This is similar to dodgeball except it involves kneeling. To begin, choose two enders for the entire game. Everyone else is in the middle. There are three primary rules. One, all players stand until they are hit by a ball thrown by an ender. Two, when someone is hit, that person must continue the game on his or her knees. Three, if hit once more, this person is out and becomes an ender. If a person catches the ball while standing, he or she can bring back in someone who is out. If a kneeling person catches the ball, she or he can then stand. "Kneel Dodge" is a fast-paced, almost nonstop activity.

LAUNDRY RELAY

RECOMMENDED GRADES:
2-12

MATERIALS NEEDED:
Laundry baskets, lots of clothes.

This activity is exciting for almost any age. Break the group into three teams. Line each team up behind a laundry basket heaped with clothing. Place a marker 25 feet away that each team must reach and run around. When the leader gives the go, the first person in each line must pick up the laundry basket full of clothing, move quickly to the marker, circle it, and return the basket to the next in line. If any laundry drops during transit, the runner must stop, pick it up, and return it to the basket. The first team to finish a complete rotation wins.

RECOMMENDED GRADES:
4-12

MAIL EXPRESS

MATERIALS NEEDED:
Packages, tables, chairs, pens.

If you need a big group competition game for 20 or more, I think you've found it. Set up tables with chairs on one side only. Have teams of ten people sit at the tables. To begin, each team receives a package that players frantically pass down the table for each player to sign. Then players sign the package again as it is passed back to the original person. Therefore, the package will eventually have two signatures from each team member. The first team to successfully complete this process wins.

RECOMMENDED GRADES:
4-12

MAKE IT OR FAKE IT

MATERIALS NEEDED:
None.

This game calls for the youths to "construct" with their bodies the object the leader calls out. First, break your group into teams of six. Second, as you call out certain words, each team attempts to construct it. A time limit can be given. Suggested objects for the teams to construct are a clock, a washing machine, stairs, a desk, and a computer, to name a few.

RECOMMENDED GRADES:
7-12

MUMMY AND DADDY

Before the group arrives, heavily toilet paper one male member and one female member of the staff. They should be covered completely, like mummies. When the group arrives, both adults will be carried out and placed in seats before the group. Next, the leader will bring out a mummified baby doll and say, "This baby is searching for its mummy and daddy." Tell the kids that the baby will not be given away until they vote to determine which of the mummies is the daddy and which is the mommy. Have the kids vote by raising their hands, then reveal which mummy is the mommy and which is the daddy. Give the baby to them if the majority chose correctly. This is a fun way to open a session.

MATERIALS NEEDED:
Lots of toilet paper, baby doll, chairs.

NAME THAT GRUNT

RECOMMENDED GRADES:
K-3

For this noise association game, invite seven kids to stand behind a hung sheet (so the group cannot see them). One kid makes a grunt sound, and one person from the large group tries to guess who made the sound. Then the second kid makes a sound, and another member of the audience attempts to guess who made it. Continue the rotation as long as it takes for the audience to guess every voice. The audience only gets one chance per rotation to guess the identity of the sound maker.

MATERIALS NEEDED:
Bed sheet, rope.

SCENT

RECOMMENDED GRADES:
8-12

If you want something that will have you smelling for hours, here it is. The purpose of this activity is to find the person in the group wearing the cologne or perfume that has been chosen for a volunteer to find. This is really a game you must put your nose into. For starters, have the group sit in a circle. Display a variety of five colognes or perfumes. Next, ask for a volunteer and have that person leave the room. Choose someone from the group to splash on one of the fragrances, then have the volunteer return. It is now the volun-

MATERIALS NEEDED:
5 varied colognes and perfumes.

teer's task to find the person wearing the fragrance. The volunteer is given only three chances to identify that person. If successful, he or she gets to keep the fragrance bottle (or splash some on). The process can now be repeated. Each time around it gets harder because more people have on a fragrance. By the game's end, it is often impossible for the volunteer to pick out the person wearing the chosen fragrance.

RECOMMENDED GRADES: 4-12

"SEE"FOOD

MATERIALS NEEDED: Food, 4 shoe boxes, square table.

Form a large circle and have all the players stand with their backs toward the center. In the center of the circle are four boxes on a table. Under one box is a bounty of food items (for instance, candy, chicken, pretzels, popcorn). When the food or snack has been hidden under one box, have the group turn to face the table. Ask a volunteer to pick up any two boxes at the same time, exposing what's underneath. If the volunteer exposes the food, the group mobs the table, takes the food, and eats it. If the food is not revealed, have the group turn around again while the box positions are switched.

RECOMMENDED GRADES: K-5

SHH!

MATERIALS NEEDED: None.

This is a fun, quick activity to quiet down a large group of kids. Through all the noise and playful activity, scream once, "Everyone who can hear my voice repeat after me." Then dramatically utter, "SHH." Some will follow the lead. Repeat until you know you have the attention of the whole group. Now the fun begins. "SHH" in different ways and patterns, and have the kids follow. "Shh, SHH, Shh, SHHHHHH, shhhh." Do this fast, slow, silent, loud, or fake until the group is coaxed into being seated quietly.

STOP AND DRINK

RECOMMENDED GRADES:
8-12

To begin, seat everyone in a circle and give them each a cup. Choose someone from the group to pass her or his cup in a clockwise direction to the next person, who stacks person one's cup on top of his or hers. Players continue stacking cups until the leader says, "Stop and drink!" The person caught with the large stack of cups must fill the top cup with soda and attempt to drink it by holding the bottom cup to guide the others. NOTE: If the players have all stacked their cups before the leader says, "Stop and drink!" they continue to pass the stack, removing the cups from the stack one by one until the leader says the needed phrase. This can be a messy, but funny game.

MATERIALS NEEDED:
Plastic cups, soda.

TALENT SEARCH

RECOMMENDED GRADES:
7-12

This can't-lose activity is overwhelmingly popular among city youths and works especially well if you are working with youths in a housing development. A talent search is the equivalent of a talent show with one difference—everyone wins. Teens who want to perform before an audience using their gifts sign up with the leader. You may want to set some rules as to what the youths perform. Most will find that city youths are great performers, actors, and musicians. Let them know up front this isn't a competition. Once all the groups have performed, have them come back out to receive some symbol of your appreciation of their performances. Encourage them to pursue their gifts and talents in a positive manner. Consider having a talent search on a monthly basis. After a while, many groups might want to perform.

MATERIALS NEEDED:
Stage, microphones.

RECOMMENDED GRADES: 7-12

TELEPHONE BOOK RELAY

MATERIALS NEEDED: Telephone books, chairs, paper pieces.

This is a race of skill and quickness. To begin this activity, split the young people into three even-numbered groups. Have each group form a line. Twenty feet ahead of each group is a chair with a telephone book placed upon it. When the leader signals the game to begin, each player is given a person or business to find in the telephone book. Each person races to her or his telephone book and seeks the information the leader requested. When it is found, the player races back and utters his or her finding to the leader. If correct, that player goes to the end of the line and person two continues the process. A player giving incorrect information must return to the phone book and find what was asked for. The first team to complete one rotation wins.

RECOMMENDED GRADES: 5-12

TILE DANCE

MATERIALS NEEDED: A tile floor or individual tiles, boom box.

This activity determines who can dance the most creatively in a space as small as a tile. To begin, assign each person in the group a tile on the floor to stand on. If you have a floor without tiles, hand out tiles for people to stand on. When the boom box is turned on, everyone dances for two minutes on his or her tile, while the leader and other appointed judges walk around and observe. When the time is up, have the judges tell their choice for most creative tile dancer.

You can make more of an event of this by having other categories like most creative on one leg, using one arm, using only hips, using only the head, or using only the lower body. One thing is for sure—when it is over, your youths will be exhausted!

Outdoor Games for Small Groups

CHAPTER 5

ANNA BANANA

RECOMMENDED
GRADES:
3-12

In this activity, jumpers attempt to catch a jump rope between their legs. While the jump rope is being turned and the jumper is jumping, the following phrase is chanted by the rope turners: "Anna Banana, play that piana, all you have to do, is squash that banana, Anna . . . Banana . . . Split!" When the word *split* is said, the jumper must stop and have the rope caught between her or his legs.

MATERIALS NEEDED:
Jump rope.

BASKETBALL SPIN CONTEST

RECOMMENDED
GRADES:
8-12

This is a contest for those who believe they can spin a basketball for long periods of time on just about everything. Begin by giving all participants a basketball. Tell them the person who has the longest accu-

MATERIALS NEEDED:
Basketballs.

mulated spin time from all categories wins. There are ten spinning categories: on a finger, a hand, a foot, a knee, the head, the ground, an arm, the stomach, a chair, and on someone else's finger. Announce a big prize for the winner, and young men will flock for a chance.

BOTTLE DRAG

**MATERIALS
NEEDED:
Thin ropes,
16-ounce glass
bottles, dirt.**

Here is an activity you can really get your legs into. This team race involves dragging bottles that are tied around the racers' legs. Be sure this game is played on a dirt lot so the glass bottles don't break during the race. First, take the bottles and tie a rope around the necks tightly. Next, split each team into two groups, and have the first person in each group tie the bottles around her or his legs. A marker should be set up 20 feet ahead of each group. When the leader signals the race to begin, each person runs around the marker and back to his or her line as quickly as possible. When the runners reach the lines, they must untie the bottles for the next people in line to continue the race. The first team to complete a rotation wins. This game is absolutely hilarious to watch.

CARTRIDGE HORSESHOES

**MATERIALS
NEEDED:
Typewriter car-
tridges (for
example, Smith
Corona Series H,
Olympia ESW
3000, Panasonic
KX-P145).**

Many games created by city kids are improvisations of other activities. Because the resources needed for the activity are beyond their means, they modify resources. This is such an activity. "Cartridge Horseshoes" is executed like conventional horseshoes, only typewriter cartridges are used in place

OLYMPIA ESW
3000

of horseshoes. Typewriter cartridges can often be found near office buildings. Many offices will give you cartridges if you ask. This activity is fun and inexpensive. Some have even used this activity to further the idea of recycling.

CHICKEN EATING CONTEST

RECOMMENDED GRADES:
6-12

MATERIALS NEEDED: Chicken.

Gather a few hungry and exhausted youths and challenge them to a "Chicken Eating Contest." The objective isn't to see who can eat the most pieces of chicken, but who can eat the quickest. Display five pieces of chicken before each of three challengers. Say, "Go!" and let them go at it. The first one finished is the champion chicken eater. The amount of chicken you have determines how many rounds you go. This is a fun interlude at a picnic with your youths.

DOUBLE DUTCH

RECOMMENDED GRADES:
4-12

MATERIALS NEEDED: Jump ropes.

This is an exciting, quick-paced jump rope activity that many urban girls play. The objective is to see who can jump between the ropes the longest. Three people are needed with two ropes (or more popular, a clothesline) between them. One rope is spun clockwise, the other counterclockwise. The ropes are staggered by a half turn; so when one rope is going up, the other is coming down. Jumpers entering the ropes need excellent coordination. Jumpers takes turns to see who can "withstand the ropes" the longest.

DUMPSTER HEAVE

RECOMMENDED GRADES:
9-12

Two Dumpsters and an open lot are needed. A team of two people

MATERIALS NEEDED: Wheeled trash Dumpsters.

race a second team pushing Dumpsters 50 feet. The first team to reach the finish line wins. The challenge comes in directing the Dumpster—what results is similar to a farmer pushing a mule.

RECOMMENDED GRADES: 7-12

EGG IN MOUTH RELAY

MATERIALS NEEDED: Raw eggs, tables, pails.

To begin this game, youths pair off as teams. One person gets on the shoulders of the other. The leader gives each team six eggs, which may be placed on a table. When the leader begins the game, the bottom person passes an egg up. The top person holds the egg in his or her mouth, while the bottom person walks briskly to a pail or box 30 feet ahead. When the pair reaches the pail, the top person passes the unbroken egg down to the bottom person, who carefully sets it in the pail without breaking it. The team returns to its table and attempts to bring another egg to the pail in the same manner. The winning team is the team that can safely transfer the most eggs the quickest. This relay is comical, especially if the top person is an uncontrollable laugher. Often the egg never makes it to the pail because the top person laughs the egg out of his or her mouth onto the head of the bottom person.

RECOMMENDED GRADES: 7-10

FILL THE BUCKET

MATERIALS NEEDED: Buckets, water balloons, ruler.

Have each individual stand about 12 feet away from the wall. Next, place a bucket at the wall for each individual. Give each person 20 water balloons. When the leader says, "Go!" the players throw water balloons at the wall low enough so the water spills into the buckets when the balloons explode. The person who has the most water in his or her bucket wins. Measure the water levels with a ruler.

FIND THE AIR HORN

RECOMMENDED
GRADES:
5-7

MATERIALS NEEDED:
Air horn.

The objective is to find the leader who has the air horn. Sounds simple, but here's the catch. The leader with the air horn has a three-minute head start to evade the kids. When the three minutes are up, the leader blows the air horn signaling the game to begin.

The young people try to find the leader as quickly as possible. However, the leader may move from the first spot. But every two minutes, wherever the leader is, he or she must blow the air horn. The first young person to find the leader wins. To gather the troops, give a prolonged blow on the air horn until everyone finds you, and play it again if you want.

HIGH-RISER

RECOMMENDED
GRADES:
7-12

MATERIALS NEEDED:
Baseball.

This game must be played outside a high-rise housing development. The purpose of this game is to determine who can throw a baseball the highest. The height of each throw is determined by the floor the ball reaches. Two judges stand 50 feet away from the group where they can objectively view how high each throw goes in relation to the building. Once the judges are in place, the game can begin. The person who can throw the baseball the highest wins. Rematch any ties.

HOBO

RECOMMENDED
GRADES:
3-10

MATERIALS NEEDED:
Bed sheets, random supplies.

This game determines who can stuff the most items in a sheet and carry it 50 feet. To begin, provide every participant with a bed sheet and a large pile of random supplies (pots, pans, bottles, books, and so on). Be sure each pile has more items than can be placed in the bed sheet. When the leader says, "Go!" each person must stuff the bed sheet with as many items as he or she can and travel a premarked distance of 50 feet within two minutes. The person who has transported the most items within that time wins.

RECOMMENDED
GRADES:
All

KICK THE BUTT

**MATERIALS
NEEDED:**
Cigarette butts,
trash can.

This activity is best done while waiting for a bus with one or two youths. The purpose is to find as many cigarette butts as you can before the bus comes. Set a goal for yourselves (like 50 butts) and attempt to find that many before the bus comes. Remember to choose beforehand where your collected butts will go (a trash can or sewer, for instance).

RECOMMENDED
GRADES:
10-12

NO DRINKING AT THE BAR

**MATERIALS
NEEDED:**
Glasses, water.

This is an extremely funny activity for the big mouths of your group. Invite four guzzling challengers to each grab a glass, already full of water. Tell them they are to drink the water in their glasses as quickly as possible. However, when the leader yells, "BAR!" the guzzling must cease immediately. The one who stops drinking the quickest is the round winner.

RECOMMENDED
GRADES:
6-12

O'CLOCK

**MATERIALS
NEEDED:**
None.

To begin, two volunteers pick a time they want the group to guess. Let's say the time picked is 10:30 a.m. The volunteers give the group one clue—the last two numbers of the chosen time. In this case, it is 30. The players in the group then bid, one at a time, until the specific time is guessed. The person who guesses the time correctly then chooses one of the categories in the following rhyme, which is chanted by the group:

> Ice cream, cake, or candy,
> Movie stars are dandy,
> Monkey in the zoo,
> Looks just like you.

After choosing one of the categories, the volunteers will create a hard question that comes from that category. If answered correctly, 1,000 points are given to the player who guessed the correct time. Choose two new volunteers, and the process can continue. This game can last a long time.

OVER THE HEAD TOSS

RECOMMENDED GRADES: **7-12**

For this water balloon race, have your group pair off. Each pair receives eight water balloons. The team's goal is to get the water balloons one by one to a box or pail 30 feet ahead of it. One member of the pair stands behind the other, both facing toward the pail. The back person tosses a balloon over the head of the front person for him or her to catch. If the balloon is successfully caught, the rear person moves ahead of the front person, who then tosses the balloon as before for the new front person to catch. The pair continues to toss and switch until it gets the balloon to the pail. If a balloon bursts in the process, the pair must return, get another balloon, and attempt to get it to the pail. The pair who gets the most balloons to its pail wins.

MATERIALS NEEDED:
Water balloons, boxes or pails.

RECOMMENDED
GRADES:
6-12

PIGEON

**MATERIALS
NEEDED:**
Masking tape.

This game requires the kids to mimic pigeons, which have a habit of not moving out of danger until the last second. Two volunteers are needed: the "pigeon" and the "car." To begin, tape two lines on the floor at the end of the room. The first line is eight feet from the wall; the second is 16 feet from the wall. The pigeon stoops on the eight-foot marker while the car races toward the pigeon from the far side of the play area. The pigeon cannot move until the car rushes over the 16-foot marker. At this point, the pigeon must rush away before it is hit by the car.

RECOMMENDED
GRADES:
5-12

PUSH-UP CHALLENGE

**MATERIALS
NEEDED:**
Water balloons.

In this challenge, the loser is all wet—literally. Two opponents challenge each other to determine who can do the most push-ups. Push-ups are to be done in a courteous fashion—when one person completes a push-up, the other will proceed. There are ten water balloons under each person. Consequently, the person with the least amount of staying power gets very wet.

RECOMMENDED
GRADES:
10-12

ROCK PUT

**MATERIALS
NEEDED:**
One rock,
weighing 15
pounds.

This activity is for the strongmen of the group. The object of the game is the same as shot put, except you use a heavy rock instead of a steel ball. The rock should be as round as possible. This activity determines who can "rock put" the farthest. Once a winner is found, a new round can take place.

RUG RAT RACE

RECOMMENDED
GRADES:
3-7

Each team races to a marker 40 feet away and returns. Sounds easy enough, but not if you are using rug squares. To begin, break the group into pairs that each receive three rug squares. Determine which child will be the front person and which the back person. The front person during the race will put down the rug squares, while the back person must pick them up and give them to the front person, who will lay them back down. The pair must also be standing on two of the three rug squares while the game is in progress. Once the race has begun, the first team to return to the starting point wins.

MATERIALS NEEDED:
Carpet squares.

SHOE TIE FLY

RECOMMENDED
GRADES:
3-7

In this relay, the winning team is the one that ties and unties shoes the quickest. This game works best with ten to 16 people. First, move to an area where it is safe for kids to walk without shoes, and divide the group into two teams. All players remove their shoes. Anyone who has shoes with laces must take them to the front. Next, give each team the same amount of shoes, making sure the shoes are untied, and place them in front of each team, at a distance of ten feet. Have the two teams form straight lines. When the leader signals the game to begin, the first person runs up and begins to tie each pair of shoes in front of his or her team as quickly as possible. When finished with the pile, the player goes to the end of the line. The next person in line then *unties* all the shoes; the person after that ties the shoes, and so on. This continues until everyone on each team has had a turn. The first team to complete one rotation is declared the victor.

MATERIALS NEEDED:
Shoes with laces.

RECOMMENDED
GRADES:
5-8

SHOOT THE CREAM

**MATERIALS
NEEDED:**
Hand mirrors,
water guns, a
can of whipped
cream topping.

Break the group into pairs. One person of each pair possesses a water gun and a mirror; the other person has the whipped cream. In this race, the person with the whipped cream sprays a three-inch pile into her or his hand. The person with the water gun attempts to shoot the cream off the outstretched hand of his or her teammate while facing away from that person. This is why the mirror is needed. The team that can spray the pile off first, without running out of water, wins.

RECOMMENDED
GRADES:
5-12

SNOW STEPS

**MATERIALS
NEEDED:**
Snowballs,
steps.

On a snowy day, have each player make 15 snowballs near a set of steps. Players attempt to hit each step in succession with a snowball. Since there are only 15 snowballs per person, it's remarkable if anyone ever makes it to the tenth step. The person who gets to the highest step is declared the winner. The leader should decide how far the players stand away from the steps, depending on the ages of the kids.

RECOMMENDED
GRADES:
5-9

SQUEEZE THE LEMON

**MATERIALS
NEEDED:**
Sliding board.

This is a popular game among city kids. To begin, have one volunteer be the "lemon." The lemon sits securely on the bottom of the sliding board braced to resist others who slide down. When the lemon is secure, the others slide down the board one at a time, providing more and more weight, until the lemon is squeezed off.

SQUIRREL CHASE

RECOMMENDED
GRADES:
K-4

Form teams of two and place each group at a tree; the larger the tree, the better. One of the two kids is chosen to be "It." "It" is the chaser. The entire chase takes place around the tree. When the leader signals the game to start, "It" attempts to catch the other person by chasing her or him around the tree. If a large tree is used, this game takes on characteristics of a squirrel avoiding a hunter. When someone is caught, that person becomes "It."

MATERIALS NEEDED:
Trees.

STEP INTELLIGENCE

RECOMMENDED
GRADES:
6-12

This is a race to see who can get to the top step first by way of intellect. Ten steps are needed. All the young people stand at the bottom of the steps and proceed upward a step at a time each time they answer a question correctly. A series of at least 20 questions must be written in advance, keyed to the level of your youths. The first person to the top wins.

MATERIALS NEEDED:
Steps, written questions.

SUBWAY ADVANCE

RECOMMENDED
GRADES:
5-9

This activity can be done on a long subway train ride. Assign partners to everyone. The objective is this: Every time the train stops, partners attempt to run to the next car forward before the doors close. Begin by getting on the last car, and attempt to board the first car before you reach your stop. NOTE: Partners should not get on the car ahead until they're sure they *both* can make it together. If a pair misses the car, another subway train will come along soon.

MATERIALS NEEDED:
None.

TICKLE MONSTER

MATERIALS NEEDED:
None.

Five leaders are needed for this game. Leaders huddle together to secretly choose which one or more of them will be the "Tickle Monster." Leaders then spread out in the playing area. On the signal, "Go!" the children run to any of the leaders and stand close to them. When all the children are standing close to a leader, the designated leader shouts, "Tickle, monster, tickle." When children hear this command, they must all try to run away from the leaders. The tickle monsters begin to tickle any child nearby. If a child escapes, a tickle monster chases after him or her until all the kids have been tickled.

TRACK WHACK

MATERIALS NEEDED:
Abandoned train tracks, tennis ball, coin.

Ideal for ten to 16 people, this game must never take place on train tracks that are still used—they must be completely unused. Split your group into two teams, then have each team stand in a line on the outside of the abandoned tracks facing the opposing team. Place a 15-foot gap between the two teams. Next, flip a coin to determine the team that will get possession of the ball. When this is determined, the first person in each line stands within the tracks. The purpose is to see who can kick the tennis ball past the other without the ball going out of the tracks. When the ball passes an opponent, it is a goal for the kicker and is worth five points. If the ball goes out of the tracks, however, the person who kicked it will have a half point taken from his or her team's total. After a goal has been successfully achieved by one of the two contenders, the losing team gets possession of the ball and then player two from each line enters the tracks to play. The team with the most points after one rotation wins.

TUG CHALLENGE

RECOMMENDED
GRADES:
K-4

In "Tug Challenge," one person takes on the group. To begin, the leader ties the rope around his or her waist. One by one the kids grab the rope and attempt to drag the leader a premarked distance and thus win the game. The objective is to see how many children it takes to move their leader. If the leader can drag all the kids, however, the leader wins.

MATERIALS NEEDED:
Tug rope.

WATER PRESSURE

RECOMMENDED
GRADES:
4-7

In the heat of the summer, this is a cool and refreshing activity to do with kids. First, you must have access to an activated fire hydrant (many cities allow this). Next, turn the hydrant on full blast. Now the game can begin. The objective is to see who can walk the farthest into the water stream without the pressure stopping him or her. The one who can proceed the deepest into the stream wins. The process can repeat itself many times.

MATERIALS NEEDED:
Fire hydrant.

Outdoor Games for Large Groups

6 CHAPTER

AIRPORT SCAVENGER HUNT

RECOMMENDED GRADES:
8-12

This activity is not only fun, it is educational because many city kids have no concept of what is at the airport except airplanes and pilots. Split the teens and staff into at least two teams. Allow one hour to complete this hunt. Each team receives a sheet of questions that must be answered or tasks that must be done before returning. Each correct answer or completed task is worth 1,000 points. Teams that return late are penalized 500 points. Below are typical items to obtain or questions you can ask.

MATERIALS NEEDED: Writing paper, pens.

1. Get a pilot's signature.
2. How many gallons of gas does a 747 hold?
3. Get a plane ticket receipt. What is this?
4. Get a flight attendant's signature.
5. Write down five airline names.

6. Get the signature of someone from another country.
7. What is the destination of TWA's flight [pick a flight number from the airport monitor]?
8. Compare rental car costs. What is the price of the cheapest car?
9. Compare rates for a flight to Hawaii. What is the cheapest rate?
10. What year was the airport built?

RECOMMENDED
GRADES:
6-12

BIG GROUP RACE

**MATERIALS
NEEDED:**
None.

The "Big Group Race" is lots of fun for a massive group outdoors. First, have the kids form groups of 15 and link arms in a circle. At the signal to begin, the groups must all move as quickly as possible to the finish line 60 feet away. The first team to successfully cross the finish line together is the victor. There is also the option of making the teams do a complete revolution. This activity is hilarious to watch.

RECOMMENDED
GRADES:
5-12

CARD STACKING RELAY

**MATERIALS
NEEDED:**
Glue, decks of playing cards, card tables.

Play this game outdoors with teams of four. Provide each team with a table, a deck of cards, and glue. It is the objective of each team to construct a building out of the cards within five minutes. The group that has the highest edifice built in that time is the winner. Sounds easy—not so! Wind is often a factor. Many players can never get their stacking any higher than three levels. The glue is an aid to construction, but the wind usually wins.

CUSTER'S LAST STAND

RECOMMENDED
GRADES:
7-12

This game follows the outline of "King of the Hill," except it is not an individual fight but a group struggle to reach the top of the hill and thereby defeat the opposing team. This game is excellent for groups of 30 to 50.

To begin, split the group into two teams. Each team member must be given a flag or marker to wear for team identification. The teams must then choose three generals apiece. Each general should be given an obvious color or smock to wear for identification. After the generals are chosen, each team must come up with a strategy to get its generals safely to the top of the hill without being touched by members of the other team. If they are touched, they are out. Each team has three objectives.

1. To set up a defensive strategy that will get the generals safely on top of the hill.
2. To get as many generals to the hilltop as possible. The team that can get the most generals to the apex in five minutes wins.
3. To set up a offensive strategy that will attempt to attack the generals of the other team.

When this game ends, the winners will know the meaning of "struggling to the top."

MATERIALS NEEDED:
A hill, colored rags, colored smocks.

DANCE TILL YOU DROP

RECOMMENDED
GRADES:
5-12

This is a dance contest—not to determine the best dancer, but to determine who can dance the longest. Gather the participants and tell them a special prize will be awarded to the one dancing the longest. Then ask the D.J. to begin. The young people will then proceed to dance . . . and dance . . . and dance, until they drop. The one who dances nonstop the longest wins.

MATERIALS NEEDED:
Boom box, a prize.

DRENCH

**MATERIALS
NEEDED:**
Fire hydrant or
water hose,
water buckets.

This is a massive water game. Either a fire hydrant or a water hose must be available. First, split your big group into two teams. Each team should have the same number of buckets. Second, each group chooses a king and a queen. Third, when the leader signals the start, it is the objective of each team to drench the king and queen of the opposing team. Each team must form a way to protect its royalty. The first team to successfully drench both king and queen wins. The more people participating in this game, the better. Be assured the teens will begin dry, but end up drenched.

DRUG DEAL

**MATERIALS
NEEDED:**
Paper pieces.

In this outdoor mystery activity, the "police" find the "drug dealers" and arrest them. At least 20 people are needed. Divide the group into three teams and move each team to a place where it can be briefed without other teams overhearing. Group one is the police, group two the drug dealers, and group three the pedestrians.

Group one, the police, must secretly find out who the drug dealers are and apprehend them. A jail spot should be chosen. Tell the team members they should work together as undercover agents. The drug dealers will try to sell drugs to the pedestrians, but the police must stop them. Also, the police must know how many drug dealers there are.

The members of group two, the drug dealers, are each given five small pieces of paper. These pieces represent the substance they are pushing. Their objective is to avoid police; if caught, they go to jail and the game is over for them. They must also try to get rid of their drugs (paper pieces) by pushing them on the pedestrians. They must now come up with a scheme to avoid police and warn one another of suspected or known police agents.

Group three, the pedestrians, are to simply walk around and do as they please, but they must be told there are both drug dealers and police agents around. Tell them drug dealers will try to sell them drugs. It is up to them whether or not they buy. Police might also question them for information. It is up to them whether or not they participate. Let them know, however, if they buy a drug, they can be arrested if caught.

Tell all the players they have free access to a three-block radius. Set a maximum time for the activity to run. Then dismiss each group in two-minute intervals.

Another option is to have the police focus on recovering all the drug slips from either the drug dealers or the pedestrians who bought them.

DUMB SCHOOL

RECOMMENDED GRADES:
3-12

MATERIALS NEEDED:
Small rubber ball, 12 large steps.

This is a favorite among many urban youths. It is a race to see who can get to the 12th step first. To start, everyone must line up at the base of the steps. The leader hides a ball in one hand. The rules are simple: Those who guess which hand the ball is in progress upward one step; those who guess incorrectly are demoted one step. The first one to the 12th step wins.

FRIGID BASEBALL

RECOMMENDED GRADES:
8-12

MATERIALS NEEDED:
Baseball equipment, hot chocolate, thermal containers.

Here's an idea for the youth group that loves baseball. The rules and objectives are the same as for any baseball game. The only difference is you play the game when it is cold outside. On a winter day, have a baseball tournament with all the kids from your youth group. Provide plenty of hot drinks to keep everyone warm, then play ball!

HALF GALLON FOOTBALL

**MATERIALS
NEEDED:**
Half gallon milk
cartons.

A low-cost alternative to football, "Half Gallon Football" is similar to tag football. Use an empty half gallon milk carton for your football (have three or four extras on hand just in case one gets smashed). Since the carton is not aerodynamic, use only half the football field. Please reiterate to the teams that this game is tag only. Once the kids have formed two teams, the game can get underway. This is often a humbling game because many at first try to be throwing all-stars but soon figure out the carton will not cooperate.

JAIL FLAG

**MATERIALS
NEEDED:**
Sheet rags.

Divide the group into two equal-numbered teams. Designate one team to be the flag team. Give each member of this team a flag torn from old sheets or rags. The flag team members tuck the flags into their back pants waistbands. Flags should hang out at least 12 inches. The chase team members close their eyes and count to 100 by fives, to give the fleeing team a chance to hide. The chase team then runs after the fleeing team, attempting to capture prisoners by pulling their flags. Once a prisoner is caught, he or she is placed in the designated jail area. A member of the chase team guards the jail. The fleeing team can free teammates by tagging the prisoners. If freed, they receive their flags back. Once all the flags of the fleeing team have been pulled, the game is over. The chase team takes the flags and becomes the fleeing team, and the game is repeated.

MANHUNT

The play area for this hide-and-seek game is the entire community.

To start, split the group into two teams. One team must tie rags around its team members' arms for identification. When the leader says, "Go!" the rag team has two minutes to hide anywhere in the community. When the time is up, the remaining team has 30 minutes to find those who are hidden and return them to the starting point. One hundred points are given for each member found. At the end of the first 30-minute round, sound the air horn to get the group back together. The rag team switches roles and pursues the other team. The team with the most points after both rounds wins.

MATERIALS NEEDED:
Rags, air horn.

MILITIA (GROUND DODGE)

RECOMMENDED GRADES:
4-8

The rules and operation of this game are like dodgeball. However, the game is played with the participants laying on the ground. No standing, kneeling, or squatting is allowed. First, divide the kids into two teams, and have the players lay on their bellies facing each other. There should be ten feet between the teams. Flip a coin to determine who gets the ball first. The first team attempts to hit a member of the other team by rolling the ball. The opposite team can avoid the ball by rolling. If hit, you are out. An out member can only return if someone on his or her team catches an oncoming ball. If the ball is caught, the opposite team member who rolled the ball is out. If the ball is missed, the member attempting to catch it is out. This game is funniest with 20 people.

MATERIALS NEEDED:
Dodgeball, coin.

OLD MULE RACE

RECOMMENDED GRADES:
6-12

Split the youths into pairs and designate one partner as the "mule" and the other partner the "rider." Straight ahead of each team is a line of ten water balloons, one yard apart. The rider gets on the mule's back. When the signal to begin is given, the mule must move

MATERIALS NEEDED:
Water balloons, stopwatch.

as quickly as possible with the balloons going between his or her legs. The mule must travel the distance, turn around, and return to the starting point without bursting any balloons. If balloons are burst, five seconds per balloon will be taken from the team's time. The team with the best time wins.

RECOMMENDED
GRADES:
4-12

POCKETBOOK RELAY

MATERIALS NEEDED:
Purses or shopping bags, apples.

The object of this game is to see which team can successfully put all of the apples into a purse the fastest. First, form three teams of ten. Second, give the first person in each team a purse or shopping bag. Third, place 20 apples 30 feet in front of each group. Next, when the leader begins the game, the first person must run and place one apple in the pocketbook as quickly as possible and return the pocketbook to the next in line to continue the process. If any apples are dropped from the heaping pocketbook, they must be picked up in order to continue. The first team to successfully retrieve all 20 apples wins.

RECOMMENDED
GRADES:
All

RAKE RELAY

MATERIALS NEEDED:
Rakes, many leaves, many trash bags.

This activity involves lots and lots of leaves, so get plenty. To begin this activity, the young people must be broken into teams of two. Each team needs a rake and garbage bags. Each team is assigned a large pile of leaves. When the leader yells, "Go!" the teams race to see who can bag and tie their piles first.

THE RIDDLE

For this treasure hunt, divide the group into teams of five. Give each team a map consisting of riddles and questions that can direct the team to a person strategically hidden in the neighborhood. When the person is found, he or she will give the finders a final map and a riddle that when solved gives a clue to finding treasure. Have the young people hunt through the entire community to find the final treasure.

To add to the fun, place decoys that offer clues to a supposedly quicker path to the treasure. Of course, these clues only sidetrack the teams that attempt to use the information. Use such decoys as an envelope on the ground that reads, "Open: Treasure Shortcut." Other decoys are people pretending to be on to something and phony maps. In short, those who stick to the original course have the better chance of winning. This is an exciting activity that can be followed up with a discussion on the danger of shortcuts.

**MATERIALS
NEEDED:**
Paper, a treasure
gift.

ROOF LEAP

Tape five large squares, 10' x 10', on the ground. Use the diagram below to correctly set up this area. Tell the group that each square

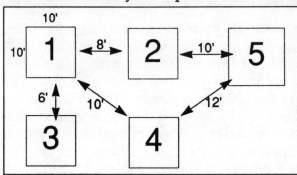

represents a rooftop. Everyone must jump from "roof" to "roof" without stepping out of the lines. A person who steps out of the lines falls off the roof—putting that person out. The kids start in square one and, with a running start,

**MATERIALS
NEEDED:**
Masking tape,
large cement
play area.

they jump one at a time into any of the five squares in any combination. Here are three possible commands: Square one to square three; square three to square two; square two to square five. Feel free to use multiple combinations or mathematical riddles—this adds to the fun. For those who are too good to be eliminated, challenge them to jump from square five to square four. If anyone can jump this distance, give that player a super prize.

RECOMMENDED
GRADES:
3-8

ROW HOUSE RUN

MATERIALS
NEEDED:
Row houses,
candy.

The purpose of this activity is to see who listens carefully enough to run to the row house identified by the leader. To begin, have the group stand in front of the corner row house. This house number will be zero. Every succeeding row house will be numbered consecutively. At the instruction of the leader, the kids must run to the house whose number is called and return as quickly as possible. The first three people and the last person will receive candy. Be creative in your instructions; for example, you must run to the house that numbers seven plus two.

RECOMMENDED
GRADES:
K-4

SCREAM CONTEST

MATERIALS
NEEDED:
None.

Here is an activity that can wake up your entire neighborhood. This activity determines who in your group has the loudest mouth. City kids love this activity. To begin, ask for four volunteers who believe they have the biggest mouths. These kids should line up side by side. The leader then gives every child the chance to scream. When the volunteers are finished, the crowd will applaud who it thinks was the loudest screamer. The winner can then be challenged by others from the crowd in an attempt to find the biggest mouth in your children's group. The winner gets the pleasure of realizing he or she is the loudest mouth.

SHOPPING CART RELAY

RECOMMENDED
GRADES:
7-12

**MATERIALS
NEEDED:**
Shopping carts.

In some housing developments, shopping carts are everywhere—use them. First, divide your group into three teams. Be sure each team has a cart. When the leader says, "Go!" the first person in line sits in the cart while the second person pushes the cart to the designated marker (30 feet ahead). When the marker is reached, the two switch places and return to give the cart to the next two players. The first team to complete one rotation is the winner.

STOMP

RECOMMENDED
GRADES:
K-4

**MATERIALS
NEEDED:**
None.

This is a spontaneous activity you can use with a large group of little kids to focus their attention up front. Begin by saying, "Do what I do." Then proceed to stomp, using rhythmic patterns; sometimes slow, sometimes fast. Use fake stomps, then soft stomps, and loud stomps. Give children patterns they can easily follow. Once you know all the children are with you, you can end.

TAKE ME TO YOUR LEADER

RECOMMENDED
GRADES:
5-8

**MATERIALS
NEEDED:**
None.

This game imagines aliens have just landed. It is the task of one person to figure out who the leader is. However, the aliens don't speak an understandable language; they communicate in tones.

For the game to begin, a volunteer must be chosen who is willing to figure out who the alien leader is. This person must then be taken somewhere away from the group so an alien leader can be chosen privately. When the alien leader has been chosen, tell the group its only response to any of the investigator's questions will be to hum.

The pitch of each person's hum will elevate depending on how close he or she is to the chosen alien leader. If across the room from the alien leader, the alien's hum will be low; if close, the hum will be high. When the investigator thinks she or he knows who the leader is, he or she will say, "Are you the leader?" If the investigator is correct, the alien will answer by saying, "Yes." If wrong, the alien will hum with a pitch according to the leader's location. The larger the size of the group, the harder it can be for the investigator.

RECOMMENDED
GRADES:
3-12

TENSION

MATERIALS
NEEDED:
None.

The purpose of this activity is to determine which young people can stand the tension of being pulled and tugged. This activity works best with ten or more. First, have the entire group hold hands in a circle. Second, when the leaders give the go, the entire group must pull as tightly as possible against each other with the intention of causing a break somewhere in the circle. When a break occurs, the two people where the break occurred must sit out. The process continues until there are one or two winners. This activity can often be followed by a discussion on the many ways people break under tension.

RECOMMENDED
GRADES:
7-12

"WHY"ATHELON

MATERIALS
NEEDED:
At least four 45-
rpm records,
paper and pens,
popcorn, books,
empty aluminum
cans, boom box.

A "Why"athelon can be constructed in various ways. Here is one with six zany activities for all to join in. At the end of the games, the kids might ask, "Why'd we even do that?" Hence the name of the game. Before beginning, explain that the players with the highest and lowest averages will win.

The first event is the record tossing contest. Everyone is given a chance to throw a 45-rpm record as far as he or she can. Event number two is the handwriting contest. Winners are chosen for the best and worst handwriting. Event number three is the popped popcorn spitting contest, which measures the distance each player can spit a piece of popped popcorn. The fourth event is the book lifting contest. Each person lifts and carries as many books as possible in one trip of five feet without dropping a single book. Event number five is the can-over-the-head toss. This event measures how far a person can throw an empty aluminum can backward over her or his head. The sixth and final event is the beat box (a rhythmic vocalization of a percussive beat). This is to see who can keep the best and worst beats while beat boxing. When the events are completed, tally the judges' results and determine the two winners (highest and lowest scores) of the "Why"athelon.

Relational Activities

CHAPTER 7

Relational activities are best played by groups of five or less, since the intention is to form intimacy and build relationships between youth workers and urban youths. City kids need to spend time with people who can talk with them about life. It is natural for a young person to receive guidance from an older person. Most kids' homes offer this by way of the immediate or extended family; however, there are still many adolescents and children who fall between the cracks. If they have no one they can turn to who can help them answer positively the questions that arise in life, they can easily turn to destructive answers (for example, drugs, sex, pornography, or gangs).

Relating with city kids on a personal basis is important. Urban youths need people they can call friends—people who are older and can give guidance. Within the urban youth subculture, role models are often missing, yet they are invaluable. A role model can be any person who is willing to spend time with a youth with the intention of guiding and training him or her to become a healthy, well-adjusted person at that particular age of development. The task of the youth worker is to become a role model of this stature.

Unfortunately, in an attempt to be a good role model, urban youth workers can fall into two traps. The first is believing there is no room for young people to play. Some youth workers want to rush kids into adulthood. Their philosophy is that things are too tough for urban youths to allow them to take time to play or relax. Therefore, to steer a life in any direction other than professionalism is not to be considered. As a result, the youth worker relates to the young person as if he or she were an adult. This sort of youth minister accepts nothing less than what he or she considers the best for the youth. With this perspective, the young person is viewed as either a success or a failure depending upon how well she or he meets the criteria of the youth worker.

The second trap is believing the only way to truly become role models for urban young people is to lower oneself to the level of the youths. This philosophy says that unless you use the words, phrases, and actions that the kids use, you really can't communicate effectively with them. You have to become like a kid yourself in order to give them good guidance.

This is an extremely dangerous attitude. Role models cannot be considered "one of the kids" for the same reason Jesus could not be considered "one of the disciples." There must be a distance of knowledge, wisdom, and age created between the youth workers and those for whom they wish to provide a model. It doesn't matter if the youth worker is 50 or 19, the individual must act his or her age. This is being a true role model, because it mirrors to youths what it means to be that particular age.

Activities that are intimate and that can be done with small numbers of young people are important in building relationships with your kids. Don't be so numbers-oriented that you lose sight of the individuals who make up the group. Make an effort to know your young people in such a way that you really do care and pray for each of them.

APPLICATION HELP

If you need an activity that really makes an impact on a young person, try aiding the teen with a college or job application. Spend an afternoon with the young person and assist with questions that arise. Many urban adolescents and children, even those from housing developments, are bright and talented. However, because of social circumstances, they have never been shown the correct way to complete a common application. A significant number of urban youths are turned away from jobs and colleges because of insufficient information on applications. The role you play is to help a young person think through every question and formulate a response that is not only intelligent but thorough.

Many urban youths don't have enough contacts to receive three professional references. You can serve as an advocate by making crucial phone calls for the teen. Let the young person know you are on her or his side 100 percent. You will earn much respect in the eyes of the young person.

MATERIALS NEEDED:
Job or college application.

BIRTHDAY ADVENTURE

RECOMMENDED
GRADES:
3-12

For urban youths, particularly those of the underclass, a birthday is the equivalent of the Fourth of July. It is treated as a national holiday. Here's an activity to do on a youth's birthday. First, plan to take a kid out on his or her birthday for the entire day. At the outset, give the kid three envelopes, explaining they contain her or his birthday present. In each envelope is a whole day of fun activities; however, the birthday person can only open one. The one he or she opens is the one you do. Be sure to include lunch and dinner in the itinerary, and do not let the youth open the other two envelopes. This could diminish his or her value of the adventure. Once all this has been taken care of, enjoy!

MATERIALS NEEDED:
Vehicle.

BUS STOP PRAYERS

MATERIALS NEEDED:
Bus stops.

This is fun to do with a few kids as you are walking a distance of ten or more blocks. The objective is to pray a one-sentence prayer at each bus stop you pass. The part of the city you are in determines how frequent the bus stops are. The best part is that little kids really get into praying. After a while, they will be running between bus corners instead of walking. This activity is great; make it fun for the kids.

BUY A BOOK

MATERIALS NEEDED:
Books.

One of the greatest favors you can do for an urban adolescent or child of the underclass is to buy that youth a book. Many of the childhood and teen classics are unknown simply because the children's parents don't buy such books. Many homes are void of any books or reading material. Children who have books around them become aware of their importance. This is why purchasing and presenting books to urban young people is a must. Often when kids win games, the prizes we give are candy or things that are not good for them. Consider giving a book as a prize. In the long run, it will be appreciated.

CLOTHES WASHING FUN

MATERIALS NEEDED:
Dirty clothes.

This activity is simple for anyone who lives near the community where he or she ministers. A few times a month, instead of washing your clothes at home, wash them at the local laundromat. Make sure to take one or two kids with you. This is a basic but most enjoyable relational activity. When you go to the laundromat, the following four things are true:

1. You have at least two hours to spend.
2. It is prime time to get to know a child.
3. It is an experience the child never forgets.
4. It relays to the child your personal interest in who he or she is.
   After all, who else would invite a kid to wash dirty clothes?

CLUBHOUSE CLUB

RECOMMENDED
GRADES:
5-7

MATERIALS NEEDED: Resources available for youths to use.

Many preteen youths, particularly boys, have leadership potential. A normal route to practicing leadership is to form a "Clubhouse Club." Ideally this is an informal group of five youths united for a specific purpose. A gang is a negative example of the same idea. To encourage the formation of a clubhouse club, realize it will usually form naturally among certain peers who are always with each other. Urban youths have two options when they become bored: to do something negative or to do something positive. This encourages something positive.

When you recognize a peer group, get them together for a meeting. Tell them you have noticed how well they work together and encourage them to form a club that will meet and do good things in their neighborhood. They would decide their own objectives. Tell them you will support them and give them resources to do activities they like. Many such groups usually want to plan trips or play neighborhood football games. Encourage this and provide what is needed for them to be successful. As this group becomes an entity of its own, the members gain incredible esteem by exercising their own abilities. Clubhouse clubs can be an asset to urban youths. The members grow confident in planning and accomplishing activities with your backing.

RECOMMENDED GRADES:
5-12

DAY LOCKUP

MATERIALS NEEDED:
Your home.

For the young person who is extremely hard to get to know, arrange to spend an entire day together, but do not go anywhere. Stay at home, watch movies, and cook dinner together. The objective is to purposely set this day up so it will force both the youth leader and the youth to create a relationship. Many urban youths who are hardest to get to know in a group will often open up when there are no peer influences. Try this activity. It may present an opening in a stressful relationship.

RECOMMENDED GRADES:
7-12

GET A LIFE

MATERIALS NEEDED:
Appointment book.

To allow urban youths to learn to organize their lives, buy a calendar/appointment book for a young person and show her or him how to use it. Tell the youth it is important to categorize his or her life and begin to set steps toward doing great things with that life. A calendar book will start the teen in this direction. Urban youths tend to have little structure or planning to their lives. This type of gift has resulted in young people who look toward the future.

RECOMMENDED GRADES:
5-12

LUNCH DATE

MATERIALS NEEDED:
None.

A great relational thing to do with urban youths is simply to take them out to lunch. It seems elementary, but when you take a young person out to lunch, you express to the youth that he or she is important to you. In short, the kids perceive you as someone who cares. A great amount of discussion and openness can result.

MAKE A CAMP BROCHURE

RECOMMENDED
GRADES:
6-12

Making a camp brochure can earn you new recruits, parental support, and perhaps donors for certain events. Too often this responsibility is left to the youth leader—it should be a shared task. Getting to know youths in a small production group can be delightful. Depending on the quality and standard of work you want, involve kids in the entire process. Have them write the copy and determine the format of the brochure. If you're running on a cheap budget, photocopy the brochure instead of having it printed. Have the youths who helped make the brochures hand them out in the community. You'll get to know kids better, and they'll feel good about a product they produced.

**MATERIALS
NEEDED:**
Paper, pencils, copy machine, typewriter.

MINISTRY BALL

RECOMMENDED
GRADES:
6-12

This is more than an activity. All urban youth workers should carry a ministry ball. A ministry ball is simply a small ball you carry with you at all times for two purposes: needed recreation or to dispel a tense sharing moment.

First, the ministry ball can be used when recreation is desperately needed. Many times when a youth worker is one-on-one with a kid, things can become boring. The ministry ball offers a source of recreation they can do together. For instance, use the ball to practice pitching, bounce it off the wall, practice grounding, throw it up in the air, play chicken against a wall, and so on. The list is endless.

The second and most important function of the ministry ball is to dispel tension. When a youth is sharing something personal and confidential that is making her or him feel awkward, the ball allows you to make the atmosphere less intense. Often when youths who are just beginning to trust their youth leader speak confidentially, they stut-

**MATERIALS
NEEDED:**
Small plastic ball.

101

ter, gasp, and "umm" because they are not sure how to put certain things into words. It is highly intimidating to a young person who is pouring his or her heart out for you to intently stare back. If you are sitting down, pull out the ministry ball and play with it in your hands or against the floor. This should be done in a quiet fashion; you want to relieve the tension of sharing, not make the youth think you're not listening.

RECOMMENDED GRADES: 8-12

MORNING ACCOUNTABILITY GROUP

MATERIALS NEEDED: None.

This activity can be the highlight of your day. Gather with a group of youths (preferably the same sex) once or twice a week in the morning before school to talk, have breakfast, and pray together. The over-arching purpose of the group is to be accountable to each other, giving the members the feeling that they're not alone when they face a struggle. Ask, "What part of this day will be the hardest for you?" You might say the 10:00 a.m. board meeting; they might say a 1:00 p.m. test. Each member in the group attempts to remember to pray for the others during their tough time of the day. This kind of accountability works incredibly well in the city, but it is a demanding commitment. Urban youths sometimes bring incredible problems that you must be willing to suffer through (for instance, a family member who is drug dependent, sexual problems, emotional scars, or death by murder). Do not sell this group short because you don't have time to be held accountable or to help a member. Great blessings can emerge from such groups.

RECOMMENDED GRADES: All

MUSIC LESSONS

Many urban ministries are looking for teachers who can train urban young people in a skill. Music lessons are an excellent place to start.

Urban young people lack musical skills not because of disinterest, but because they have no resources to take lessons. Children showing musical talent are often self-taught. If you have an instrument and time, share your gift. Watching a child turn on to music is a wonderful thing.

MATERIALS NEEDED:
Musical instruments.

OUT FOR THE DAY

RECOMMENDED GRADES:
5-12

Many adolescents and children view their youth director as a zany, crazy, fun individual who does nothing but have fun all day long. They do not realize that a director's job involves planning, making phone calls, and attending meetings. This activity encourages you to ask a kid to tag along with you for part of your day to see what you do. Meetings are the best. If you do nothing else, take a kid to a meeting with you. Let the youth see how meetings are run and how people plan together and negotiate. For urban youths, it is often a new experience, plus they get to see you in a different role. Afterward, solicit the kid's response to some of the issues you were facing in the meeting. Kids love giving their opinions. By the end of the day, you will have a young person who knows more about your work, and you will know more about her or him.

MATERIALS NEEDED:
An itinerary.

PRAYER CHAIN

RECOMMENDED GRADES:
5-12

This is a ongoing activity for a small group of youths and their youth pastor. Many struggling urban youth pastors find it hard to do anything with kids except the normal youth meetings. Once a week, gather a group of five or less together to pray. Allow everyone to give the group something to pray about until you meet the next time. Then get together the following week to praise God for all he has answered and to bring up new prayer issues. This can be very rewarding for both the youth pastor and the youths.

MATERIALS NEEDED:
None.

RECOMMENDED
GRADES:
All

SPENDING TIME WITH A NOBODY

**MATERIALS
NEEDED:**

None.

Some urban youths have so many past or present problems that they feel they are nothing and have nothing to contribute. Choose one or two of these youths to pour as much time into as you can. Attempting to be Superman will wear you out, so don't try more than two youths. Often these kids have more needs than you can meet. Don't attempt to win them over miraculously in two weeks or two months, and don't try to make them into what you want. Allow them the range to become who they can be. Certain kids will always be nerdy. It is your duty to make that nerd believe in himself, instead of creating a fictitious "cool" guy who is a nerd.

RECOMMENDED
GRADES:
5-12

TURNABOUT IS FAIR PLAY

**MATERIALS
NEEDED:**

None.

The urban youth worker usually spends massive amounts of money on the young people he or she works with, often leading to the conclusion that he or she has been manipulated—and this is exactly what happened! Often youths usurp funds by pretending to be much less stable economically than is true. Therefore, the sitting duck to make things better is the youth worker. This is sometimes acceptable, but not always.

This activity encourages the young people to do something nice for the youth worker. Express to a few of your young people that you are fed up with constantly spending money every time you do an activity together. It is now time for them to do something nice for you. You will be surprised at the response. The young people who have an appreciation for what you do for them will offer to take you to get an ice cream, treat you to a movie, or invite you to dinner. This type of activity is healthy for your youth group. The best groups do not constantly take from their leaders; they often give.

Educational Activities

8

CHAPTER

Activities that are created for education are instructional games. Instructional games are created so that urban young people will have the chance to think openly and critically on topics that concern and influence them. As is often noted, city kids have ideas and insights into many of the topics that concern them today, but rarely have a creative means to express that insight.

For example, urban graffiti is often seen as an eyesore or as nonproductive. This is true—defacing of property in any form is wrong and destructive. However, what is graffiti to graffitists? It is art. They see what they do as a means of expressing themselves artistically, rather than as defacing property. There are city youths who have exceptional talents and gifts. But without the means to express themselves in an appropriate creative way, they will use these talents destructively.

It is the task of educational games and activities to create an atmosphere that allows children and adolescents to express their creative abilities and use them for constructive means. Educational activities are a must. They are a basis for us to teach themes and subjects that ought to be learned.

If we are to seriously approach the field of urban youth ministry, it must be from the angle of education, not just from the angle of fun. I feel this is crucial. Education on the issues that face urban youths (for example, drugs, illiteracy, gangs, sexuality, self-esteem) is a point on which all urban youth workers must unite. Educational activities help urban youths to creatively grapple with many of their contemporary circumstances.

RECOMMENDED
GRADES:
1-3

ABC SCAVENGER HUNT

**MATERIALS
NEEDED:**
Cut letters from
stencils.

This is a wonderful educational activity that tests alphabetical and sequencing knowledge. It is best if done with one to three kids. First hide every letter in the alphabet around the room or building. When the leader signals to begin, kids must find the scattered alphabet. However, they must find the letters in alphabetical order. If a child finds a letter that is out of order, he or she must leave it and come back to it when the other letters that lead up to it are found.

RECOMMENDED
GRADES:
8-12

ACT IT OUT

**MATERIALS
NEEDED:**
Index cards.

Set up like a game show, this activity challenges the knowledge of opponents by a series of questions that require the players to define certain words. If you fail to define the word, your opponent says, "Act it out." You are then given the definition and must act it out.

After you have determined who receives the first question, begin the game. As soon as someone fails to define a word, give that person the definition and he or she will act it out before the whole group. This is extremely educational and funny. If a word is not known, be assured it will be remembered once it is acted out.

AESOP TIME

RECOMMENDED GRADES: 1-3

This is an excellent activity for little kids who love people to read stories. This activity has the kids create a moral for each story read. Call it "Aesop Time" so kids will know its purpose. Explain that Aesop was a Greek writer of fables that always ended with an explicit moral. One example is Dr. Seuss' story, *Green Eggs and Ham*. After the reading ask, "What should be the moral of this story?" The moral the kids create for this particular book might be, "Things are not always as nasty as they seem." *The Cat in the Hat* could be deciphered as, "To let a stranger in your house could leave it a mess." Have the kids create a moral for every story. Write each moral down and hang it up. This usually ensures their attentiveness. Try this activity; it promotes creativity.

MATERIALS NEEDED: Kids' books, poster board, tape, marker.

BEAD IT

RECOMMENDED GRADES: 1-3

The purpose of this activity is to enhance color and sequencing abilities. This is a craft in which each child constructs a bead necklace. To begin, the leader starts a pattern the children must follow. This pattern should include an alignment and color sequence. For example, bead a string with this pattern: two red beads, one clear bead, one green bead, two red beads. Have the children repeat this pattern on their own strings and continue it until their strings are full. There are a multiplicity of patterns you could use, so have fun with this. The kids will often not want to stop.

MATERIALS NEEDED: Yarn or string, various colored beads.

COLLEGE TOUR

**MATERIALS
NEEDED:**
Vehicles.

One of the most successful things you can do with urban youths is to plan a college trip. Most urban kids have the minds and abilities to attend and succeed at college. For many, however, college is viewed as an impossibility.

Plan a week-long trip that will take your kids to colleges both in and out of state. Essentially, it will be a tour that exposes the young people to their many collegiate possibilities. Prepare for this activity in three phases: pretrip briefing, the tour, and posttrip debriefing.

Be sure each phase is well planned and organized or the results can be detrimental. Be sure both your staff and teens are well informed and motivated. On the trip, encourage kids to inquire deeply into the majors they are interested in. Many might never have another chance to ask so many diverse questions. Those who attempt this with urban youths will definitely find it is a success.

COLOR-O

**MATERIALS
NEEDED:**
Crayons, paper.

"Color-o" is similar to "Bingo," except it helps children learn colors and numbers. Before this game begins, draw on each page one large square with five rows or squares across and five rows or squares down. In short, it should look like a Bingo board. Next, number each space from one to 25 starting with the upper left corner. Once this is done and you have one Color-o sheet per kid, the game can begin. NOTE: It is best to have many Color-o sheets on hand, so when one game ends you can begin another.

The rules are easy. The first one to get a certain arrangement of colors in a straight line wins. Therefore, the game is leader schemed and led. The leader says to the children both a color and a number (for example, yellow-seven or purple-twelve). Using the color called, the children color the square of the number called. The first child to realize that he or she has a complete sequence of colors in a row yells, "Color-o!" and becomes the winner of that round. A new sheet can be given to repeat the game.

COUNCIL LEADERSHIP

**MATERIALS
NEEDED:**
None.

City kids need an active involvement that allows leadership. One model is the youth council. The purpose of the youth council is to establish the rules and bylaws of the larger group. They determine discipline procedures, assist in trip planning, and help make key decisions that determine the direction of the group. Council leadership acts as an advisory board to the general staff. Councils should be elected by the group, have a definite term of office, and be held accountable by the staff. This can often be a long-term education for teens. Their positions give them the opportunity to know what they can and cannot do as leaders. The specific duties of council members should at least be the following:

1. To take minutes
2. To plan trips
3. To collect trip money
4. To participate in planning youth group activities
5. To implement plans
6. To be responsible for the club rules
7. To establish discipline procedures (not oversee their execution)
8. To be a voice for their peers

Forming a council is an act of trust from the staff to the youths. When the youths are allowed the responsibility of leadership, you will be surprised at the outcome.

DINNER ETIQUETTE

**MATERIALS
NEEDED:**
Tables,
streamers,
drinking glasses,
table settings,
cake, soup,
spaghetti.

Table manners are something that must be taught. They do not come as a process of development. They must be mimicked and practiced. Sometimes in the process of urban ministry, you come across kids who have never learned table manners. Although it might not be necessary in their immediate social situation, it is a social skill that needs to be acquired. This is a fun activity that practices this skill.

Before youth group begins, set up the room like a fine restaurant. Give it a fun name like "Le Urbane Souffle." Make a small meal that can be stretched if more youths come. Have soup and spaghetti.

When the teens arrive, tell them they are entering a fine restaurant. Proper manners are required, and anyone not acting accordingly will have to leave. Assign them seating. Once everyone is seated, place one staff member at or near each table. Tell the group this activity is to see how well mannered they could be if they were visiting a fine restaurant. It is important for them to learn how not to embarrass themselves or others in these situations. Tell them they will be observed and judged as they eat and discuss. The table that is most mannerly will receive a cake, compliments of Le Urbane Souffle.

The following criteria are suggested for the judging process:

1. Posture
2. Intelligent discussion
3. Manners
4. Eating etiquette

This can be a great activity as long as the staff takes it seriously. Afterward, you could have a discussion with the youths concerning why proper public eating etiquette should be mastered.

FIREHOUSE

RECOMMENDED
GRADES:
2-5

**MATERIALS
NEEDED:**
None.

This is a good safety game for little kids. Break the group into three teams. Team one is the fire team, team two is the water team, and team three is the oil team. Tell the kids that when there is a fire, only water can put it out. On the other hand, oil makes fire burn longer.

Once the teams are divided, have the oil and water teams stand together to start the game. Have the fire team stand about 30 feet away. When the signal is given to begin, the fire team continuously yells, "Fire, fire, fire." It is the objective of the water team to get to the fire team to put the fire out. When a member of the water team touches a fire team member, that team member's flame is extinguished and that player should sit down. The objective of the oil team is to prevent the water team from reaching the fire team, thus prolonging the fire.

There is a time limit. If the water team cannot put the fire out in two minutes, the oil team wins. Teams can then switch roles.

FIRST AID RELAY

RECOMMENDED
GRADES:
4-7

**MATERIALS
NEEDED:**
None.

If you are interested in teaching the principles of first aid to city kids, this is an exciting activity. However, it requires some preparation on your part. The Red Cross, a local school, or a certified staff member must teach these principles. This relay is a test to determine how much the kids have learned from their training in first aid.

The competition element doesn't really matter in this activity. The overall purpose is to see what the kids can remember by learning from each other. Divide the group into three teams. The leader stands 30 feet in front of the teams. When the leader gives the go, the first kid in each line runs to huddle around the leader. The leader gives the kids a question about first aid. When someone knows the answer, he or she says it aloud. The other ones who weren't as quick to respond then repeat the answer. All three kids run back so the next group can run up. In short, the race always comes down to the last runners. Once the race is over, compliment the group for all stating the answers.

FLASH SENTENCE

MATERIALS NEEDED:
Index cards.

This is a great activity for children who have just begun to learn how to sequence words into sentences. The concept is similar to flash cards. First, write out a sentence on index cards. There should be one word per card. Next, scramble the cards and have the kids unscramble them into a coherent sentence. This can be done to teach sentence structure to little kids and as a race for older kids.

FOR SHAPES ONLY

MATERIALS NEEDED:
Cardboard or construction paper.

This activity follows the principles of "Red Light, Green Light." Groups of ten to 15 make this game fun. Squares, rectangles, triangles, and circles must be cut out of construction paper or cardboard. Give each child a shape. Now the game can begin.

The children all line up against a wall. The leader starts each time by saying, "Green light for . . ." then a shape will be yelled out. The children with that shape must quickly walk forward until the leader yells, "Red light!" When this is heard, those moving must freeze or they will be sent back to the wall. This repetitive activity is great to help kids visually learn about shapes.

GOOD TO GO

RECOMMENDED GRADES:
K-4

This activity provides children a method of gauging their behavioral performance. Those who are good will be able to leave first; those who aren't will leave later. On large poster board, list downward every child's name. Across the top, list behavioral categories. Below are some suggestions.

MATERIALS NEEDED:
Poster board, marker.

1. Courteous
2. Comes prepared
3. Finishes homework
4. Raises hand
5. Does not disturb others
6. Cleans area
7. No eating or drinking
8. Helps others when finished with homework

Each category is worth 100 points. The leader must decide how many points each child has gained from each category. The points must be counted and a list produced reflecting the amount of points gained by each child. At the end of the session, dismiss the children according to the amount of points gained, and encourage those with lesser points to do better tomorrow.

GRADES-ARE-UP DINNER

RECOMMENDED GRADES:
5-12

Many urban young people miss a grade before they reach grade 12. Usually when kids "fail," this label follows them for life. This activity combats this.

A "Grades-Are-Up Dinner" is for those youths who have successfully passed a repeated grade. These kids have beat the odds, and they

MATERIALS NEEDED:
Prepared dinner.

should be told that. This dinner can be as simple as inviting these kids to your house for a meal, or you can have a formal dinner where a speaker is invited in to encourage the young people.

Activities like this are necessary. No matter which model of dinner you choose, young people must be told they are breaking the odds by passing with such spiritedness. Encourage them to continue. Go as far as giving graduation scholarships to those who hang in there and complete all 12 grades.

<table><tr><td>RECOMMENDED GRADES:
K-2</td><td># GUESS-O</td></tr></table>

MATERIALS NEEDED:
None.

This activity is for kids who are just beginning to associate words with letters. The object of this game is to guess the first letter of a given word. If you want, you can count how many times someone responds correctly, and reward a winner. First, the leader says a word to the group. Second, the children raise their hands if they believe they know what letter the word begins with. Third, the child you choose must give you the correct answer or you will choose another. For example, let's say the chosen word is *elephant*, and a child says *elephant* begins with an "l." Gently correct the child, then ask if someone else knows what letter *elephant* begins with.

<table><tr><td>RECOMMENDED GRADES:
K-4</td><td># HEALTH NUT</td></tr></table>

MATERIALS NEEDED:
Different types of edible nuts.

This activity explains the value of nuts as an alternative snack. Many urban youths have nutritionally inadequate diets. Dedicate a week or a month to eating right. Tell the kids no candy is allowed into the group during this time. Use each session to learn about a different type of nut (where it grows, what it is called, what makes it different from other nuts). At the end of the session, eat that nut for a snack. Kids love it.

JUST SAY, "WHOA"

MATERIALS NEEDED: Writing paper, pens, poster board, marker.

This discussion game concerns an alternative approach to handling sexual pressure. Sexual activity among many urban youths often is a result of not learning tactical procedures for dispelling such advances.

To begin, start an open discussion on methods the kids use when someone approaches them about sexual activity. Be ready for open and honest answers. You will likely find that some have had sex before—deal with it. Ask them to express what led up to it (if they are willing to talk about it). Was it because they were pressured or was it a personal choice?

After an opening discussion, form groups of ten or less, separating males and females. Have each group make two lists. The first list should be lines that are used by your gender group to try to pressure someone of the opposite sex into a sexual relationship. The second list should contain lines that can be used by a youth being pressured into unwanted sexual activity. Once this is completed, have each group share its conclusions. Write these out and post them up in front of the group.

Integrate into the discussion the "Just Say, 'Whoa'" philosophy. That is, if a young person is to be successful in fighting the pressure to engage in sexual activity, he or she must be willing to *stop, think,* and *react accordingly.* Stress that most sexual activity outside of marriage among Christians happens as a result of passion and not concrete thought. We must be willing to say, "Whoa" when necessary in order to control immediate passion and to think first about the consequences of these actions. Present this as a suggestion and solicit the kids' responses. This activity offers youths an alternative when responding to sexual advances.

LOTTO LOSS

**MATERIALS
NEEDED:**
3 shoe boxes,
index cards,
paper, pens,
pennies.

City people tend to spend exorbitant amounts of their income on the lottery in an attempt to get rich quick. As we know, if the person was to hold onto the money instead of spending it so frivolously, he or she would end up richer in the long run. This activity attempts to show young people how futile it is to spend money in this way, especially when you do not have much money.

To begin, stuff each of the three lottery boxes with cards numbered zero to nine. Give each person a sheet of paper and a roll of 50 pennies. The youths can keep these pennies. Anything they win, they win; anything they lose, they lose. Let them know if they bet one penny on the lottery and win, they will receive ten pennies. The concept is that they will receive ten times the amount they bet if their numbers come up. For each round, have the young people write the three digit number they think will be the winning number. Once the youths have their numbers written and displayed for you to see, shake the boxes and draw out three numbers. This will be the winning lottery number. The kids must have that number in the exact sequence that it was drawn to win; if not, they lose their bids. This game can go at least 25 to 50 rounds. Afterward, begin a discussion on the senselessness of putting your money in a system that is constructed for people to lose most, if not all, of what they put in.

MAKE YOUR OWN BILLBOARD

**MATERIALS
NEEDED:**
Construction
paper, 12" x 18"
paper, scissors.

Kids in the city are bombarded by graphic images on walls and billboards advertising liquor, cigarettes, and much more. Lead a discussion about how these images may affect them negatively. Follow this up with an opportunity to create their own billboards that advertise something positive and something godly. Have them draw or use cut paper to create a city street similar to where they live, but add a billboard larger and higher than all other objects. Let it have eye-catching appeal or a clever message based on a Scripture reference or biblical truth. This may be done individually on 12" x 18" paper or in a group on mural paper. It may be helpful to start them out with a theme.

You may decide to go in a different direction. Have students discuss some wall murals they have seen in their city—whether downtown or in their neighborhood. Then give them a chance to create a wall mural they have always wanted to see. It gives them a chance to dream and explore their own ideas. Students plan which wall in their neighborhood they would like to paint (perhaps the one with the most graffiti), then they sketch their ideas on paper. This lesson could be followed up with a vote for the favorite idea and a plan to carry it out.

MY HERO

RECOMMENDED GRADES:
3-6

MATERIALS NEEDED:
Writing paper, pencils.

City kids need good role models. Encourage them to find and interview role models for themselves in their own neighborhood. Focus your group time on these heroes. Have the kids ask each hero for a picture so you can put the photos up in an area of your meeting place called "The Gallery of Heroes." Give each child an interview sheet that includes the following questions:

1. How long have you lived in this city?
2. Tell me about your family when you were growing up.
3. Who is one person who made a big difference in your life? Why?
4. What is something that happened to you that was very important or life changing?
5. Tell me about the most fulfilling thing you have ever done.
6. Who are your heroes or people you admire?
7. What is the one thing you would like to accomplish before you die?

117

This activity allows the children exposure to people from their community who are heroes in their own ways.

MY NEIGHBORHOOD

MATERIALS NEEDED:
Library, writing paper, pens.

In most cities, kids have good access to libraries. Take some kids to the library, and give them an assignment to find a book that reminds them of their neighborhood. Once they find this book, have them read it and write down four reasons the book reminds them of their neighborhood. Afterward, talk about the items they wrote down. Make them feel good about the neighborhood.

THE NEWS REPORT

MATERIALS NEEDED:
Markers, paper, poster board.

This activity allows kids to use communication skills by preparing a news report. When the youths enter, split them into two groups of six. Tell them they are newscasters. It is their responsibility to put together a quality, ten-minute news program. To add some diversity, each group covers a topic that concerns urban youths today. Suggested topics are: teen pregnancy, drug abuse, education and the importance of goals, contemporary music, ways to make the youth group better, or the effectiveness of religion with city youths.

Give each group 15 minutes to prepare its report. Explain that everyone must have a part in this show in some form. It is best if different reporters handle different aspects of the topic in journalist form. Provide each group with markers and paper to use if needed.

After each group presents its report, discuss as a large group how informed and professional the youths seemed, then commend them on their efforts. This activity allows urban youths to intelligently present their ideas and knowledge on certain topics that concern them.

PHONICS GAME

RECOMMENDED
GRADES:
1-4

**MATERIALS
NEEDED:**
Blackboard,
chalk.

In this activity, the leader has a word the kids need to guess. There are blanks placed across the blackboard that match the length of the word. Let's say the word they must guess is *bear*. There would be four blanks on the blackboard. The first clue should be, "This word begins with the sound 'Buu, Buu.'" Pronounce the B sound. If the kids miss it, give them three clues to help narrow it down. For example, "It comes in black, brown, and white." "It is something you don't want to see in the forest." "I've seen one on Chicago's football team." If it is not guessed after the fourth clue, give the pronunciation of the last letter. Continue until the word is guessed.

SHOPPING MANAGEMENT

RECOMMENDED
GRADES:
6-12

**MATERIALS
NEEDED:**
Supermarket,
money.

This activity is designed to teach urban youths how to manage limited money. At least 16 people are needed. Break the young people into four groups. Tell the kids they have a limited amount of money with which to buy supplies for a meal. Group one is in charge of the main dish, group two is responsible for the fruit or salad, group three is to get a beverage, and group four gets the dessert.

Each group must be given an amount of money that is below the normal standard to buy enough food for the number of people you have. In short, the amount of money given will be enough to buy a meal, but the teens will have to shop around and bargain hunt in order to make it happen. Give each group no more than 20 minutes to figure out its options and be in line. Afterward, take the food items to your meeting place and make a meal.

TOUR DE NEIGHBORHOOD

**MATERIALS
NEEDED:**
Markers, poster
board, scissors,
dice, index
cards.

This is an excellent activity for an inner-city tutoring program. It is a mock bike race that encourages children in your program to accurately finish their homework assignments. This activity should take months to play. The steps to execute it follow below.

1. **Make a neighborhood map.** Make a big wall-sized map of the community in which the kids live. Draw all the streets and apartments, and be sure to mark all the homes of your kids on it. Then establish a course of travel (see map below). Draw arrows around the map to show the direction the game will take.

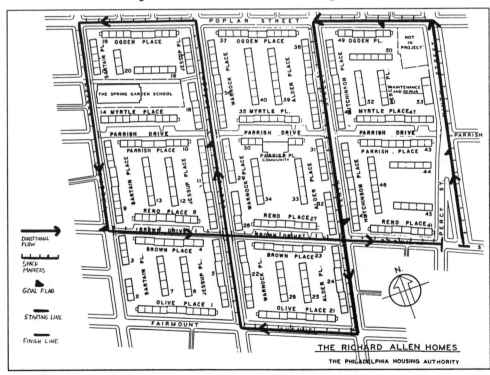

2. **Make game pieces**. Have the young people draw and color bikes on index cards then cut them out. This cutout bike serves as the individual's game piece.
3. **Place space markers on the map**. There must be 100 space markers for contestants to move their bikes on when they roll the dice. You will need both a start and a finish line.
4. **Set goal flags**. Goal flags are set on the course. The first goal flag is easy to reach, but not the rest. This emphasizes that reaching goals gets harder with each goal. Goal flags will be set on these spaces: 5, 15, 30, 50, 75, and 100. Each time a goal is passed, the child receives an educational prize (for example, pencil, pen, paper, markers, book—each specific goal should be assigned the same prize).
5. **Establish a point system**. Since this activity is to encourage young people to get their homework done accurately, there has to be a point system established. In order to be eligible to play the game, each child needs to gather 100 points to earn a roll of the dice. Points are given for each of the following: attendance, finishing homework, behavior, bringing their supplies, working quietly, getting an "A" on a test.

    Once 100 points are achieved, the child is granted a roll of the dice and can move his or her bike that many spaces. But there is also an opportunity here to choose a chance card. When the child has rolled the dice, he or she can stay with the number rolled, or the sponsor can ask, "Do you want to take a chance?" If so, then the child must stick with whatever the chance card says.
6. **Make chance cards**. There are three types of optional chance cards. *Bonus cards* allow the players extra moves. *Bad cards* (flat tire, oil slick, and tired) cause players to lose their moves for that day *Good cards* reverse bad cards (air pump, sure grip tires, and Gatorade). When players receive good cards, they can save them to use against bad cards drawn later, or they can turn them in to advance three spaces.
7. **All those who finish are rewarded**. The first person to successfully finish should be given a wonderful educational

prize (for example, a chemistry set, a microscope, a scholarship). Once everyone finishes, all players should be given the same prize (a party, dictionaries, a ream of paper).

"Tour de Neighborhood" is a splendid activity that will reap prestigious benefits within your young people. It is encouraged for any inner-city tutoring program.

RECOMMENDED
GRADES:
8-12

YOU THIEF!

**MATERIALS
NEEDED:**
Pocketbook or
wallet.

This activity is to be an object lesson. As youths arrive, have a pocketbook or wallet displayed in an area where it could easily be taken. Next, take a young person aside and explain what you are doing. Ask the youth to take and hide the pocketbook or wallet when it appears no one is looking. Then have the youth brag about it to one or two of his or her friends, yet swear them to secrecy.

After a while, begin to look disturbed and come before the group to explain that a valuable item is missing. You have searched and searched, so it must have been taken. Initially ask, "Do any of you have it? If you do and you turn it in now, there will be no penalty." Have the participating youth do nothing and pressure with his or her eyes that his friends better not. After this question fails, seemingly distraught say, "Okay, no one will leave tonight until it is returned. I will be more than glad to sleep out here tonight and tell your parents why." Then proceed to give a parental-like lecture about trust and mistrust. Threaten to cancel a trip or a youth group meeting if no one returns it. Have the participating youth continue to pressure his or her friends to not tell. See if they do.

At this point, most young people who have nothing to do with it will not want to be penalized for one person's actions and will attempt to investigate. Remember, tension will be high, especially on the one or two who know who it is. Set a time limit for this to take place—usually ten to 15 minutes. If no one tells on the culprit by this time, have the participating youth confess. Watch the group's reaction. This works even better if it is a person the group thinks is trustworthy.

At this point, let the teens in on what has really happened. Discuss their feelings, especially when they found out who it was. Ideal questions are as follows:

1. What did you think when told you might not leave?
2. How did you feel about this person's actions infringing on your freedom?
3. What did you initially think about the person who actually did it?
4. Ask those who knew who it was how pressured they felt to tell on their friend?
5. Should good friends ever tell on each other?

Family Activities

CHAPTER 9

Participating with families in activities is one of the most important things an urban youth minister can do. Among the urban underclass, families do not regularly come together for fun. This is often not possible because people are either too busy or too tired, trying to just survive. It has been my experience that if there is any prolonged family activity, it usually takes place around the television. But television is not a great family-building activity because individuals relate to it, instead of to each other.

Urban youth workers often forget the importance of relating to a child's family. Don't let this happen, particularly when parental support decreases as the child gets older. I don't know how many times I've "met" parents only by way of a signature on a trip permission slip. I've spent time with parents (outside of going to their homes) only when activities or programs demanded they be present. Creating activities and games for the family unit is an invaluable way to increase support for your youth group. When you have adults behind you, you have the kids too. Parents must be met and the initiative must be yours.

Urban youth ministry has a tendency to focus only on the child; I believe our boundaries need to extend into the family. Often the secret to helping a troubled youth lies in understanding the stresses within his or her family.

Richard Allen Homes is the largest low-cost housing development in Philadelphia. There are over 1,300 living units in this community. Within the nine-square block area are many families with children struggling to survive. They believe in the potential of their community, even though it is often infested with drugs, and killings occur on an almost daily basis. The strength of this community is in the determination of its families. As a result, when I visit this community, it constantly strikes me that the basis for youth ministry is family ministry.

Finally, it is the task of this chapter to promote activities and games that encourage family unity, dignity, pride, and good relations. In the midst of doing ministry to youths, let us be mindful that they are but a part of a significant whole. Both the child and the family affect one another. Let us not lose sight of this: To minister to one without the other is a tragic waste. The urban family is a gold mine that awaits excavation.

RECOMMENDED GRADES:
All

ADOPT A KID

MATERIALS NEEDED:
None.

This activity is for the married youth minister. Kids who are neglected need someone to listen as they express their thoughts. Find a youth in your group who needs ministry from you and your family. Often the best choice is a young person who has an extremely dysfunctional family structure. For example, some kids have parents who are never home because they are trying to make ends meet; others are victims of abusive neglect. Ask the parent if you can take the youth once a week and have the child spend time with your family. Plan to do something special with this young person each week. Make the youth feel like a part of your family. NOTE: Treat the youth as you would a niece or nephew; never attempt to be the parent. This effort can often add an incredible sense of esteem and security to a child who normally would be considered a latchkey kid.

BABY BOOM

RECOMMENDED GRADES: **All**

MATERIALS NEEDED: Poster board, construction paper, markers.

Every once in a while a young person has a new arrival in his or her family—a baby. In urban youth groups, you might find that it is a youth that will be having a baby soon. This activity is for either situation. It is a celebration for the baby and the parent(s) who will have to raise that child.

After the baby is born, ask the parent(s) if the youth group can visit and spend 30 minutes or so seeing the baby and delivering a card or flowers. Pray with the parent(s) to show you care and to ask God's blessing upon the raising of the child. Bring some food with you during your visit so you won't impose upon the food resources of the family. Often the parent(s) will send a thank-you card.

DINNER DATE

RECOMMENDED GRADES: **Parents**

MATERIALS NEEDED: Food.

Many single parents work hard all day and return home to begin dinner. Call up one of these parents, and explain that you would like to make his or her dinner one evening. Tell the parent you will do absolutely everything. This will be the adult's evening to be served.

If possible, arrive and begin cooking before the parent returns from work. Have everything set up nicely. Let this parent feel like royalty. Involve his or her child in this service. Tell the parent you appreciate all she or he does raising the child. NOTE: There will be a parental tendency to do something. Let the parent do absolutely nothing. When the dinner is finished, the parent will thank you profusely. In short, you will have given that adult an evening to remember.

FAMILY DISH NIGHT

**MATERIALS
NEEDED:**
Family-prepared
meals.

This activity is geared to accentuate the culinary talents of the families from which your youths come. Every family has a dish or favorite food that is enjoyed by the family and has become a symbol of continuity and heritage.

A few weeks in advance, tell parents you're planning a "Family Dish Night" to share some of the main dishes in each family. Find out what some of these dishes are and organize it so everyone won't be planning to bring the same thing. This is always a wonderful evening getting to know parents and sharing in some of their finest meal preparations. Don't be surprised if some of the meals don't fit your palate. Family meals are always tailored to an individual family's taste—this is what makes the evening special.

FAMILY EXPENSES

**MATERIALS
NEEDED:**
Poster board,
writing paper,
pencils, markers.

This activity is geared to help urban young people understand how much is involved in running a family. These are the prime years for kids to begin experimenting with sexual activity. If a young person can correlate big expenses with having children, perhaps that knowledge can deter such behavior.

First, ask every young person to express how many children he or she wants to have when older. Most tend to say two or three. Explain that they cannot change the number of children once they pick a number. Second, they must give gender and ages to those children. Third, they must determine the occupations they want to have when they are older. They must also decide if their partners will work and the type of jobs they will have. Once this is done, the activity can begin.

The purpose of this activity is to put an estimated price on the cost of raising a child and economically maintaining a family for one year. Since actual costs fluctuate greatly, much of this activity will need to be tailored to your context. A spreadsheet should be posted that displays various categories according to family needs and family wants. The family-needs category should list food, clothing, rent, gas bill, water bill, electric bill, insurance, phone bill, and unforeseen expenses. The wants category should list going out for the evening, a vacation, car payment, buying your kids what they want (this section alone can be enormous), car gasoline, new furniture and appliances, a shopping spree, a computer, baby-sitter, and so on. This category can be extensive.

After you have a few categories listed, pick three young people to take through the process of estimating how much it will cost to operate their fictitious family units (do this in front of the larger group). Make estimates as realistic as possible, then add it up. It is best if you pick people with differing numbers of children. In this way, the group will realize how much each child taxes the family. Afterward, begin a discussion and point out that this activity assumes two parents; therefore, it would be much harder with only one. Finally, encourage the kids to go home and determine how much it costs for their immediate families to operate. They will often be surprised at the figure.

FAMILY WINDOW

MATERIALS NEEDED:
Windows, tape.

Here is a fun activity little kids love. You will need many windows. Dedicate one window to each child's family. Each child is to tape up pictures, photographs, and other reminders of his or her family. During one session, have each child explain to the group all of the items in her or his window and how they are family related. Make the children proud of these windows and honored to be a part of the families from which they come.

RECOMMENDED
GRADES:
3-12

GUESS WHO'S COMING TO VISIT?

**MATERIALS
NEEDED:**
Refreshments.

Instead of inviting the family to the youth group, take the youth group to the family. Ask a family of one of the youths if it could host the youth group one evening. Let the family be the main attraction. Ask the parents if they could share for about half an hour about their family. Ask them to share family stories, secrets, and photo albums with the young people. Let the family know how much this will benefit the youths.

After the family shares, pray for the family and its existence. Urban youths need to hear and see operating families regardless of their shapes or sizes. Refreshments should follow. Either bring your own refreshments or reimburse the parents for their generosity.

RECOMMENDED
GRADES:
4-12

HEIRLOOM NIGHT

**MATERIALS
NEEDED:**
A youth group heirloom to be chosen by the leader.

Heirlooms are passed down through generations to let each individual know she or he carries the tradition of those who came before. Ask the kids to bring a family heirloom to "Heirloom Night." The heirlooms are to be displayed, and each youth must share with the group what the heirloom means to his or her family circle. Have the kids share stories about their families and other heirlooms or traditions they have. Before the youths leave, display an heirloom you want to dedicate to the youth group that will be handed down to each youth group that follows. The heirloom can be serious or funny.

RECOMMENDED
GRADES:
All

HOMEBOY

The particular advantage for an urban youth minister working in a housing development is that when a youth is sick, he or she can be

MATERIALS NEEDED:
Poster board, markers.

visited with ease. When a member gets sick and cannot come to the youth group, put the child on a sick and shut-in list called "homeboy" or "homegirl." Make a card for the youth, make a card for his or her family, and give a get-well-soon cupcake. At the beginning of your youth group, take 20 minutes and go to the sick member's home. Tell the parents that because their child is sick, you have made a card for both of them and want to give a cupcake to wish the child a speedy recovery. Sing a song, have a prayer, and head back to youth group.

MY BLUEPRINT

RECOMMENDED GRADES:
2-4

MATERIALS NEEDED:
Paper.

The purpose of this activity is to allow kids to determine how much they are like their parents and which side they favor. In short, the youths will find out the parental blueprint from which they come. Some city kids may not have ever met one of their parents, so they will have to rely on one parent as a resource, or they can use another family member (aunt, uncle, grandparent).

The following questions should be given to the kids on a sheet of paper to take home for investigation:

PART I: My Outside Blueprint
  1. My eyes are like which parent?
  2. My ears are like which parent?
  3. My nose favors which parent?
  4. My hair favors which parent?
  5. My complexion favors which parent?
  6. My body build is closer to which parent?
  7. My eyebrows favor which parent?
  8. My lips favor which parent?
  9. Which parent am I more like outside?

PART II: My Inside Blueprint
1. When I am angry, which parent am I like?
2. When I am happy, which parent am I like?
3. Which parent am I like when alone?
4. My sense of humor is comparable to which parent?
5. The way I talk sounds like which parent?
6. The way I laugh sounds like which parent?
7. Which parent am I more like inside?

When the children return these questions in the next session, ask them to explain what it was like asking their parents these questions. Was it fun or not? Then go over each question and remind the children that they are a combined blueprint of their parents as God intended for them. Make them proud to be a product of their parents.

RECOMMENDED GRADES: K-3

MY MOMMY IS . . .

MATERIALS NEEDED: None.

This activity allows little children to identify what they love about their parents. Have kids form a circle. Go around the circle and have each kid start with this statement, "My mommy is. . . ." The children have to end the sentence with something they love about their mothers. Go around the circle a few times and, if time permits, you can change the statement to, "My daddy is. . . ." NOTE: Some city kids do not have a father who lives with them or they have no memory of their fathers. So be ready to change gears or supplement if a problem or negative chord arises.

RECOMMENDED GRADES: 7-12

OLD BUT NOT COLD

Many urban nursing homes are filled with people who have been abandoned by their families. This activity provides urban youths the ability to become a family to elderly people who have no family.

Contact a nursing home and explain to the head overseer that your group would like to make a monthly commitment to visit this nursing home. Impress upon the young people the urgency of showing love to those who do not have people who care about them as a family. It is now the group's role to be a family to those who have no family. Spend an hour or two visiting and encouraging the aged. Make a card for each person that says, "You are my family." The cards will be given to the elderly residents.

MATERIALS NEEDED:
A nursing home, white paper, markers.

OUR HERITAGE

RECOMMENDED GRADES:
6-12

Many city kids do not know their family histories. This activity promotes a little research. Plan to invite to the youth group at least two families who will be highlighted and will share their histories. When youths and families arrive, give each family poster board. Ask the guests to make a family tree, going back as far as they can. Have them list as many names or events as possible that have influenced the family line to now. When this is done, have each family share with the youth group the people who are on the chart and how they are significant. After each family shares, open it up to questions from the youths. Have some pocket questions that will keep discussion flowing. To conclude, have the rest of the kids tell about what they know of their families, and encourage them to go home and ask more about family heritage.

MATERIALS NEEDED:
Poster board, markers.

PARENTS' NIGHT OUT

RECOMMENDED GRADES:
Parents

Here is a one-night service you can offer that promotes parental concern. If you have a large staff, plan a "Parents' Night Out" evening. This is an evening where parents can transfer the concern for their children and go out. Many urban parents, particularly those of the

MATERIALS NEEDED:
Vehicles.

underclass, cannot get out to enjoy a nice evening once in a while, simply because of their parental responsibilities.

For starters, plan a fine evening for the parents (for example, a dinner or a play). Next, contact some parents of children in your program and invite them to this evening. Tell them they have nothing to worry about as far as their children are concerned because two of your staff members will baby-sit that evening. Use this event to get to know parents personally. Allow them an evening where they are special. Let them know you appreciate what they are doing with their kids and that you will pray for them. Once the evening is over, give the parents your number and tell them they can call you if they have any questions concerning the youth group. This will be a tremendous evening for both the parents and your youth organization.

<table><tr><td>RECOMMENDED GRADES:
7-12</td><td>**ROLE SWITCH**</td></tr></table>

MATERIALS NEEDED:
None.

Tell the kids a week ahead of time that the following week will include an activity for both youths and parents. When kids and parents arrive, tell them to sit together. If any youths arrive without their parents, they will help staff with questions.

This game is modeled on *The Newlywed Game*, but there is no competition. The youths will portray their parents and the parents will portray the youths. The objective is to see how each group will answer questions when the roles are switched. This is where it becomes interesting, because they begin to get a perspective of how each views the other. When asking questions, refer to the parent as "child" and the child as "parent." Sample questions that cause creative tension are as follows:

1. How old should your "child" be before she or he can date? Why?
2. Role-play what the parent/child dialogue would be if the "child" was to return home drunk.

3. Ask the "child" what type of person he or she wants to bring home for the "parent's" review?
4. Ask the "parent" to tell the group about her or his "child" from birth to now.
5. Ask the "child" to share two personal things that nobody knows.
6. Have the parent/child team role-play a typical day from morning until evening.

These questions always bring forth hilarious discussion. Make this activity fun. Give parents and children a chance to realize they need to understand each other more.

THE VERY FIRST TIME WE MET

RECOMMENDED GRADES:
7-12

MATERIALS NEEDED: None.

Often urban young people live in families that rarely discuss the bond of love between the two parents. It is assumed by all, but rarely uttered. This is an option for the kids to recognize the love that exists between their parents by looking at where it all began. NOTE: This activity is usually shared within family walls, so the youth leader must either encourage the young people to stimulate this discussion when they are home or invite the parents to the youth group.

The following questions are to be asked of the parental couple:

1. What do you remember about the very first time you met?
2. Who was more interested in the other? Why?
3. Describe your first real date.
4. What was your first impression of each other's parents?
5. Why did you decide on the names you chose for your kids?
6. Why did you decide to raise kids in this city?
7. If you could do it over again, what would be different? What would remain the same?

This is an excellent table discussion that produces laughter and creative introspection. It is a must for every kid to hear and know the basis on which her or his nuclear family stands.

THIS OLD BLOCK

**MATERIALS
NEEDED:**
Old
photographs.

Most urban housing developments have a rich family history. This activity allows young people to take pride in the families of the community by taking a look at the evolution of the community over the years and the families that have been crucial in its development. Begin by inviting in key people from the community who have been there for many years. Ask them to bring any old photographs they have of the community and the families. Pass these photographs around so the children will get an idea of the way things were. Have the visitors share stories about the community's past and the families that have come and gone. Allow the young people to ask questions of these people. This activity is an excellent way to have the kids realize that families are the basis of every good community.

WHO IS MY FATHER?

**MATERIALS
NEEDED:**
Writing paper,
pencils, Bibles.

This activity is strictly for urban children and adolescents who have very negative emotions toward their fathers. Because of the missing male image in some families, many urban young people have extremely deep hurts and anger that arise when their fathers are mentioned.

Give each member a piece of paper. Ask the youths to respond honestly to the following questions:

1. When you think of your father, what one word comes to mind?
2. How often do you see or hear from your father?
3. Do you know where your father is?

4. What age were you when you first realized you were angry at your father?
5. Write at least two reasons you think your father is not with you.
6. If he was to come to you tomorrow and ask you to forgive him for all he has done in the past, would you forgive him? Why or why not?
7. Do you often keep this anger in or do you attempt to express it to others?
8. Who in the world reminds you of your father?
9. From what you know or from what you have heard from others, how are you and your father alike?

After the youths have finished responding to these questions, discuss each one. Kids need to hear that others have some of the same feelings they do. NOTE: Do not force any young person to join the discussion if he or she is not willing.

Next, let the group read in succession Exodus 20:12 and Ephesians 6:1-3. Afterward, challenge the group with this question, "Should a person honor a parent who does not honor the child?" Allow this issue to be openly discussed. When this discussion is over, begin to inject the Christian motive of forgiveness. Ask pointed questions that link forgiveness with the feelings youths have toward their fathers. The leader must push the importance of Christian forgiveness because it is the element of freedom for their feelings. Read Colossians 3:12-21. Have the youths write down personal ways they can forgive their fathers for having hurt them. If any youths still cannot forgive, respect it. Don't make a child forgive. But it is your duty to let them know what Jesus requires. End the session with a comforting prayer. This is a sensitive issue, so please enter into discussion with that in mind.

Political Activities

10
CHAPTER

Political activities are necessary for urban youths to develop as socially-conscious individuals. The society in which most urban youths live is affected on a daily basis by the decisions and policies of others. Urban young people must be made aware of the social forces and individuals that politically enslave or liberate them. The social freedom of urban youths is predicated upon knowledge of present circumstances.

It sometimes seems a conspiracy that society makes provisions for the progress of only some of its constituents. It is true that the disenfranchisement of the urban underclass can be blamed on both the individuals and on our society. As urban youth workers, we should strive to make our youth groups as politically conscious as possible. When we attempt this, we need to be sure it is on a level that the young people can understand.

What urban youths must understand is that there is structural evil that invades our society. If they want hope, they must become the needed elements of love, justice, and action. Urban young people need to comprehend the inner workings of the political system so that they might be able to contribute to positive social change. It is a tragedy to see young people who don't believe they can make any difference in their community. This is generally rooted in broken political promises from those who use the underclass on their way to the top. If city kids aren't convinced while they are young that they have some say politically, it becomes almost impossible to convince them of this when they are older.

I was once at a community meeting in a housing development that was gearing up to renovate the community. This meeting was pivotal to the residents who cared about the progression of their neighborhood. After a while, an older man entered the room; he appeared to be in his early sixties. As he sat down, the dialogue continued about what power the community had to cure its own social ills. The conversation facilitator made a statement: "Stop depending on the city to give you everything. We now have the money and resources to renovate this neighborhood. The money's in our hands! No one can take it from us. It is now our time to claim our own. We have the power to reclaim this neighborhood; we can, we will. We have the power—now!"

This disturbed the older gentleman. He spoke out, "I don't understand. Who's really in charge of the changes?" The facilitator said back, "You are!" The man stopped to think about that statement, but could not absorb it. He proceeded to ask the question again, but in mid-sentence the facilitator shouted, "Do you not understand? For once in your life, this community now has the power to control its own destiny. No one else can tell you about these renovations. We have the money! We do the hiring, we do the firing. We decide who will be our architects for the renovations." Then the facilitator stopped, looked directly into the man's eyes with great intensity, and softly made this statement, "Don't worry, I understand. You never had the power to control your community or your own destiny. Well, I have come to tell you—you now have the power."

It still was hard, but the gentleman was slowly beginning to realize that he actually had the ability to effect political change. There was a noticeable tear in his eye, and all I could think of was the prophetic statement of Amos, "Let justice roll down like mighty waters and righteousness like a mighty stream."

Urban youth workers must start now to convince city teens and children that they can make a difference politically in their own communities and in the world.

AIDS REVIVAL

This activity is extremely controversial, but can be a statement to your church and society. In many churches, kids have the liberty of planning a week-long youth revival. Speakers are invited to challenge the souls and minds of the young people. The purpose is usually to have the Gospel preached to youths. Each evening an offering is usually collected that is often given to the church. In this instance, however, designate the funds collected during the week to be given to a local AIDS clinic. This will definitely get the ear of the press. Invite the press to interview some of the youths. This will let the larger community see that the youths of your church care enough to do something about what many consider irrational, even immoral. This should be the stance of your youth group: God created everyone to feel love. The revival has taught us that we need to put the Gospel into action. Some of the most unloved people in this country are AIDS patients. We want to show the love of Jesus to these patients by showing we care enough to give to cure their disease. We believe if Jesus was in our place, he would do the same thing.

What must be understood are the four distinct steps. The first step is the revival itself, which is to be strictly sermons preached. You come to learn, "Thus sayeth the Lord." Second, the offering is your mission. You want to give it to AIDS patients. The third step is to tell the press of this unusual mission. However, the press is not really necessary. The fourth and last step is to have the youths themselves take the money collected to the center they have chosen. This is the completion of the mission. NOTE: The youth director must be sure these four distinctions are definite. It will give the youths the best experience and will allow a good basis to explain your objectives.

RECOMMENDED
GRADES:
5-12

BOYCOTT

**MATERIALS
NEEDED:**
Typing paper,
typewriter.

Occasionally there are formal organizations that blatantly take advantage of urban individuals. People who are incited by these incidents often do not know how to formally exercise their right to protest. Some popular urban boycotts are aimed at local businesses that discriminate, law firms that are vulturous, police brutality, banks that redline particular communities, or individuals in the neighborhood who bring degradation upon the community, to name just a few. The impetus does not have to begin with adults; it can begin with youths.

There are steps to follow, however. First, in some cities a permit to strike must be obtained. Second, a letter must be sent to the business stating your demands and your striking intentions. It must be stated, however, that the strike will not be called if reconciliation is made with your group before the date of the strike. Third, a week before the strike, the press must be informed by letter of your intentions and demands. Fourth, once the strike begins, it must end at the time your group stated.

If you are to do a boycott with youths, it should take one of two forms. In the first form of boycott, your group confronts the business or individual you are boycotting mostly by letter with the intent to reconcile. The initial step in any boycott is to write a formal letter to the party stating your specific grievances and reservations pertaining to the actions or policies of the business.

Next, you must communicate a deadline for the party to either respond to your letter or change the policy, or you will formalize a true boycott. If the party responds to your youth group cordially and convinces the group that good measures will be taken, end with a preboycott victory. If the response is negative, boycott. Draft another letter stating that as of a certain date, your group will no longer support the organization and will encourage others in the same manner until this policy is changed. NOTE: The process must be done by the youths, not the leader. The leader should be the brain behind it all, but the workers must be the young people or your boycott will not be genuine.

The process can end at this first step or you can take your grievances one step further—a public strike. This is the second form of boycott your group can back. The youth group must understand that the purpose is not to strike forever, but to bring public attention to the specific injustice that is being perpetrated by the business or individual. Therefore, a youth strike should never be any longer than a few hours. Whenever kids are united against an injustice, it will gain attention, so notify both television and newspaper press.

When your boycott is over, have a celebration with your youths for a job well done. Encourage them to continue the private boycott until policies have changed.

CAP COLLECTION

RECOMMENDED GRADES: 7-12

MATERIALS NEEDED:
Trash bags, gloves, poster board, markers, camera.

This is a cleanup activity that can be used for promotional purposes or can be done in conjunction with the police or a political representative. If your young people are growing up in an environment where drug abuse is the norm, a cap collection is appropriate. This is a collection drive to gather as many empty cocaine/crack vials as possible within a week and to present them to the local police. Set a goal. In some neighborhoods, it would not be unrealistic to make your goal 500 vials. Before you begin this activity, you must stress the following to your youths:

1. Always wear gloves when collecting the vials, and wash your hands immediately afterward.
2. Never take a cap off an empty vial (there is occasionally cocaine

residue inside).
3. Collect these vials in a bag. Do not stuff them in your pockets.

The following explains what the activity involves and shows how it can become promotional:

1. Involve the local political representative before the activity starts. Politically this is a wonderful bargaining chip. Tell the representative this event can be used as a part of the next campaign if he or she provides gloves and trash bags for your group. Invite him or her to come help. The representative can also get you press coverage, whereby you could make statements thanking the representative for giving the supplies necessary to make the event possible.
2. When the youths bring these articles in, there must be a secure and safe place to put them until the week is over. The youth director must determine this place.
3. Take some photographs of all the contents together. Make a few posters with these photographs on them and put them around the neighborhood. The posters should send an antidrug message and express that the photographs were taken in the same community.
4. Gather all the vials together in bags and invite the local police to come and collect your cleanup effort. Tell them you did not want to put the vials in the normal trash process because of the contents. They will come immediately.
5. This activity is a rarity among urban youths, so the press could use it as a feature article or editorial.

This activity is definitely a way for urban youths to see the amount of drugs that are used in one week by their community. Continue to instill in them the determination to stay off drugs and to do good instead of evil.

DON'T TRASH WITH ME

**MATERIALS
NEEDED:**
Trash bags, trash
cans, gloves,
camera.

The purpose of this activity is to get the attention of the local political representative. As with many urban neighborhoods or housing developments, trash is a common eyesore. The goal of this activity is to convince the youths that they can make a significant change in their community. There are two ways to go about this.

The first way works if your local political representative is with and for the people of the community. Contact him or her and explain that your youth group will be cleaning up the community and wants this to be a plus for the representative's next campaign. The only thing you want from the politician are the resources for the cleanup (for example, trash bags, trash cans, gloves). Ask for press coverage, which can be used later for his or her campaign.

Plan B is appropriate if your local representative is insensitive to the people and you want to get her or his attention. Plan a "Don't Trash with Me" cleanup campaign aimed at the representative's insensitivity on this issue. First take photos of the condition of the community before the cleanup and invite the press to the campaign. Collect as many bags of trash as you can. Pile them high upon each other. Take photos of the community conditions after the cleanup. Mail the representative the pictures you took with a letter expressing your concerns and the conditions of your campaign. The conditions should be that the youths will stop their campaign and help the representative's cause as soon as a commitment to clean up the neighborhood is made. Depending on the intensity of your campaign, let your kids stop if the representative will commit to furnishing your youth group with adequate supplies to clean the neighborhood periodically. In turn, this can be credited to the politician's next campaign.

**MATERIALS
NEEDED:**
Banner cloth.

DRUG PARADE

An impressive activity for a large urban church camp or group is to have a march on drugs throughout the neighborhood. Teach the group about drugs and why they are evil. This should be a part of the curriculum weeks before the event takes place. To prepare for the march, inquire if a permit is needed or if any neighborhood committees must give clearance. Second, invite the press and political representatives to take part in this activity. Last, this march should not take place unless the safety of the youths can be ensured. This can be done with both community adults and police. One week before the march, have the group make antidrug banners that will be carried during the march. This activity makes a statement to drug users and dealers.

**MATERIALS
NEEDED:**
Writing paper,
pencils, poster
board, markers.

FEMINIST MANIFESTO

This activity allows the girls of the group to express politically those things that the boys of the group do to tacitly oppress them. To initiate this activity, separate the girls from the boys. Then announce that this youth group, like most every other organization, has been sexist in many ways. Then express that something must be done now. Allow the girls 15 minutes to privately discuss changes that need to be made in the group or things that should be altered. Have them write their suggested changes down and bring the list to the larger group as their "Feminist Manifesto." When the girls return, list their manifesto on large paper. Then announce these rules will be adopted as a part of the group unless there is any question that needs further explanation. Be assured questions will arise from the boys' side.

A debate will soon arise about feminism and fairness. Guide this conversation constructively and lead both sides to an agreement about what is fair in the group. NOTE: If the staff leadership is male, you may be in for a surprise yourself. The girls might think you need to step down more often and let your female staff members do more; you must be ready to comply with this. End by completing the negotiated draft of the manifesto, and display it somewhere in the room where you meet. This is a wonderful activity that sparks political discussion and directly affects youth group policy.

GOD AND GOVERNMENT

RECOMMENDED GRADES:
8-12

MATERIALS NEEDED:
Paper, pencils.

Begin by explaining how the United States government is based on the principle of separation of church and state. Give the reasons our government did this, and discuss the advantages and disadvantages. Then tell the teens they have just been chosen to be a fictitious advisory board to the United States government. The government wants advice on whether God should be more involved with the governmental affairs of our nation.

Next, break the group into teams of five. Ask them to discuss the following three questions and then make a final proposal that they will state to the group.

1. How important should God be in the affairs of government?
2. What large societal changes are needed to make God a larger factor?
3. How would these changes affect each type of individual (rich, poor, intelligent, handicapped)?

Have each team present its final proposal, and then you write them all down. Thank the group for wrestling with this issue. If suggestions are good, send them to your local congressman.

RECOMMENDED GRADES:
9-12

HOMELESSNESS VIDEO

MATERIALS NEEDED:
Video camera, video cartridge.

Here is a good activity for an urban church setting. The purpose of this activity is to make a video to be shown to the larger congregation that represents the tragedy of homelessness. This will allow youths to genuinely deal with this issue because they must construct a production that is reflective of this topic.

Give them guidelines on what the production should include in order to be appropriate to show at the church. The following are typical guidelines:

1. The video must contain at least two interviews with homeless people.
2. Some facts, figures, or statistics should be mentioned.
3. Express needs you see.
4. Give some solutions as you see them.
5. The video must include related Scripture.
6. A plea should be made to the audience to help in some definite way to do away with this social evil.

The production of such a video should be spread out into a four-week period. The youth pastor should review the youths' intentions and give guidance where necessary. The best guidance is to remind your group to call shelters for interviews. Often the young people desire to go directly to the streets, overlooking shelters. Break the group up into teams that will deal with each particular aspect of the video. This will allow for a better final product. If at all possible, do not use any professional machinery to produce this. There will be no cut material, so they will have to do the best they can. This will force them to categorize and organize what is essential to this video. If there are blunders, they will remain uncut.

Finally, when the production is completed, have the entire group review it. It will be a hit. If the final product receives the approval of the youth pastor, then it should be shown to the church body.

HOMOSEXUAL AWARENESS

RECOMMENDED
GRADES:
8-12

**MATERIALS
NEEDED:**
Writing paper,
pencils, poster
board, markers.

Since this is a controversial topic, this is a controversial game. Homosexuality is a topic that is often shunned by the church, primarily because it has not been dealt with theologically. On the other hand, this is a hot topic in politics. The purpose of this activity is to allow young people to look closely at how different this country would be if it were under the leadership of a homosexual majority. Both positive and negative aspects will be viewed.

This activity has four parts. In the first part, break your group into teams of four. Give each small group a sheet of paper. On this sheet, each group must write ten things that would be different if this country had been founded by homosexuals. Give them ten minutes. Afterward, list the conclusions of each group. Briefly discuss these to be sure the kids understand the full implications of their statements.

In the second part, each group has to visualize itself as a defense attorney defending the constitutional rights of homosexuals before the Supreme Court. Each group must formulate a three-point argument to be presented to the entire assembly of youths. Each group will have ten minutes to formulate and practice its presentation. The group with the best presentation will win a prize. This will ensure the kids are serious about their presentations. Have each group give its presentation and have a staff member choose a winner.

The third part is another court presentation, but this time each group must formulate a three-point argument expressing the views that the Christian church should have toward homosexuals. Afterward, discuss why the church has had a problem choosing a stance on this issue. Talk scripturally and sensitively to allow the youths to formulate their own ideas.

The fourth and last part challenges the youths to Christian service. Ask them, "What are five things we can do this year to educate ourselves both politically and religiously on the issue of homosexuality?" Write their responses on the poster board before the group. Decide on one idea you can start immediately and form a small committee dedicated to working on this.

RECOMMENDED
GRADES:
1-4

INJUSTICE GAME

**MATERIALS
NEEDED:**
None.

The object of this game is for little kids to get a sense of what injustice is. This game is simple to execute. Make two teams, but have one team be twice as big as the other. The game you play is unimportant. What matters is that the game be favored for a majority—the larger team should win every time. After a while, the smaller team will feel cheated and that the game is unfair. Play along by saying, "You can do it, keep going." Once the smaller team is about ready to give up, end the game and sit everyone down.

Begin to lead a discussion on why the smaller team felt cheated. Although there are many forms of injustice, introduce injustice to the group as a majority who has an unfair advantage over a minority that has to play twice as hard to even attempt to win.

RECOMMENDED
GRADES:
7-12

KU KLUX KLAN MARCH

**MATERIALS
NEEDED:**
Writing paper,
pens.

In the past decade, the Ku Klux Klan has reemerged publicly. Usually they plan a membership rally that is highly publicized or plan a march that will take place somewhere in the city or surrounding area. Make your youths aware of racial injustice by participating in the anti-Klan rally. Before you go, your group should consider doing one of the following: write a letter to the Klan leaders or hold a session to learn more about their philosophy.

While at the rally, carry signs that are constructive in content. It is important that the young people learn that even if they have anger toward this group, it must be expressed in a tactful and Christian manner. Since such events usually have a tense atmosphere, the following must be reviewed with the group:

1. Everyone must wear a similar color for identification in a mass rally.
2. Everyone must stay together at all times.
3. Any unseemly behavior will not be tolerated within the group, nor will we participate in such behavior.
4. If safety is breached, we will leave immediately.

This can be an activity that will thrust your youths into social action. This experience is never forgotten and challenges kids to make a stand against injustice.

LETTER TO A SOLDIER

RECOMMENDED GRADES: **1-6**

MATERIALS NEEDED: Poster board, stamps, construction paper, letter paper.

Among the urban underclass, a significant number of eligible young adults choose to enter military service, primarily because it is a way of progressing out of the community as a hero. This activity allows little kids to write some of those community heroes. To begin, find a few names and addresses of young adults who have entered military service from the community. Then have the children write a letter and make something to send with it. The letter should express why the group is writing the soldier as a neighborhood hero. Second, ask that a letter responding to the kids be mailed back to the group. Third, ask for a picture of the soldier and some pictures or an item from where the adult has been. Fourth, ask if the soldier minds if the group keeps writing her or him periodically. Last, ask if the soldier will come talk to the group when next home on leave.

When the soldier writes back, read and display the letter to the group. Display any items that might have been sent. If the soldier is ever on leave and is able to come visit the group, treat him or her like the hero the soldier is. Kids love heroes; give them real ones instead of television ones.

THE MAJORITY DOESN'T ALWAYS WIN

**MATERIALS
NEEDED:**
None.

This activity is used to introduce the topic of South African apartheid. Within South Africa, it would seem the majority African population would have the upper hand. Not so. Because of the power that the white minority possesses, the majority African body has had extreme difficulty in breaking the shackles of apartheid.

This game is constructed so that the majority will almost always lose. To begin, make one-fourth of your group the minority team, while the remaining people will be the majority team. Next, the majority team members are told they must try to attack the minority team by forcing them to the ground. But the minority team has an advantage. If its members point at any individual approaching them and say, "You there . . . bang!" the majority team member must fall to the ground inactive. This continues until one team is victorious. It is almost always the minority team that wins. The game can be repeated many times to see if the majority team can ever improve itself tactically. Afterward, correlate the unfair power advantage of the minority team to win over the majority team with tactics used to oppress the South African majority. Be assured this activity does not deal with all the issues of South Africa, but it is a visual alternative to express the effects of power inequality.

MANAGEMENT APPRECIATION DAY

Most government low-cost housing developments have a management or resident council office. Doing ministry in the neighborhood can be extremely difficult without one of these two groups behind you. This activity lets them know your kids appreciate their letting your youth ministry do work in their neighborhood.

Tell the kids how important it is for the management office to feel good about their presence. Express that if it was not for the management office, many things that are done to keep up the neighborhood would not happen. In appreciation of all the managers do, guide the youth group to create a card or craft thanking the managers for anything and everything they do. Also, kindly ask if the managers would be available to come out (on a day you choose) for a "Management Appreciation Day." This will take place during the youth session. Have the managers come to tell the history of the neighborhood or to be active that day in youth group. The point of management activity is that it causes the managers to see what you do from the inside and also to feel you appreciate the efforts of the management office. This is one way to be assured almost any realistic thing you ask for your youth group will be given. Give awards to the management office staff in honor of their dedication to the community. Make a great day out of it.

MATERIALS NEEDED: Construction paper, markers.

MISREPRESENTATION CAMPAIGN

RECOMMENDED GRADES: 7-12

Every once in a while the press will print a falsehood about the particular community where your youths live or will misrepresent them in a discussion that concerns them. Neither the youths nor the community should have to put up with this. Such a negative picture is painted of these communities when the truth is that the bad minority brings judgment onto the good majority. It is your task in a "Misrepresentation Campaign" to remind the press of the good majority. The campaign should use the following procedures:

1. Cut out the offensive article and make a copy.
2. Type a letter to the paper giving the reasons it was offensive to your youth group.

MATERIALS NEEDED: Typing paper, typewriter, scissors.

3. Explain the missing aspects of the article in detail. In short, suggest what should have been said.
4. Demand reparations. You have two options to suggest to the paper. The first is to settle for a letter of apology written to the youth group explaining the paper's position. Or if the article was extensively damaging, your group has the right to demand a printed apology that will appear in the newspaper.
5. Let the newspaper know there is good in the community. Invite the reporters to come for a tour, courtesy of the youth group. This will allow the reporters to see what living in the community is like the majority of the time.

This is a beautiful way to get urban young people mobilized to protect the good image of their community. This activity must be led by the youth director as the prime negotiator in this process. Teach your young people to be proud of their community.

<table>
<tr><td>RECOMMENDED
GRADES:
5-12</td><td># MURDER WALL</td></tr>
</table>

MATERIALS NEEDED:
Wall, paint.

If you work in a drug-infested community, this might send a message to the entire community of how often the evil of drugs results in murder. Find a wall in your community that is highly visible. Paint some commemoration on it like, "Dedicated to all the residents of this community as visual evidence of how drug warfare can deteriorate our youth, our people, and our community."

The purpose of this wall is to record the casualties of drug warfare. Begin with a certain date. Every time someone from the community is killed from drug-related activity, have the youths put the victim's name on the wall. If names become substantial, people will begin to take notice. Often visual aids like this can be the beginning of community drug salvation. Some walls number from 50 to 100 names.

THE OVERGROUND TIMES

RECOMMENDED GRADES: 10-12

MATERIALS NEEDED: Paper, typewriter, copier machine.

This is a newspaper produced by the youths on a monthly basis. A newspaper can be one of the best tools to introduce urban kids to the politics that control their lives, and this can be an extremely liberating activity.

To produce this paper, there must first be a dedication to it by the young people. The overall purpose of "The Overground Times" is to print articles that socially or politically influence the lives of young people. Articles can range from "Why the Elevators Don't Work" to "Ten Good Reasons Good People Live Here." The issues that will be written or considered must arise from those things that are directly affecting the young people or the community from which they come. When the paper loses this aspect, it loses what it was created for. "Overground" should mean unearthing the issues that have tacitly been covered over and exposing them to the fresh air of public scrutiny.

Every youth worker must keep in mind how radical such a paper can become. It must be kept contained and integral. Allow no issue to be prepared slanderously. Great things can often come of this type of paper. Often the residents cannot wait for its arrival.

PUBLIC SERVICE ANNOUNCEMENT

RECOMMENDED GRADES: 8-12

MATERIALS NEEDED: Typing paper, typewriter.

Most television stations offer the public the ability to give public service announcements. This is a platform for those people and groups that have an opinion and want to intelligently express it on television. This can be an advantageous platform for your youth group to express a political opinion. The general process is as follows:

1. Type exactly what you and your group want to say during the public service announcement. Your presentation must be as

objective as possible. Usually you are given one minute.

2. Mail this announcement to as many television stations as possible. This is to assure you a better chance at being chosen. The first television station to respond will be the station you will speak out on.

Try this to help express the group's political views. When youths know they have an opportunity to make a difference, they do.

RUNNING FOR MAYOR

**MATERIALS
NEEDED:**
None.

This activity is for a large group. Choose beforehand two candidates who will run against each other to become "mayor." Choose people whose views are different; this makes for a good campaign. As the group enters, announce there will be a mock election to determine who will be mayor. Tell the kids the importance of choosing someone who will represent their views rather than just choosing someone who is presently popular. Let the group know there will be a debate during which the youths can ask questions of the candidates. Once the debate has finished, a vote will be taken to determine the mayor. Ask questions on issues that are actually facing the city and that all mayoral candidates must answer. Ask moral questions as well. Put these two candidates through the grind. Then let their peers question them. When questions seem exhausted, give the candidates an opportunity for final statements. Finally, have the vote and announce the winner.

WHAT IS LIFE?

This activity is meant to educate urban teens and children about the controversial issue of abortion. There is a high pregnancy rate among city youths that makes abortion an issue they might have to face. They need to formulate now where they are going to stand on this religious and political issue. This activity should be executed in two phases.

MATERIALS
NEEDED:
Poster board,
markers, writing
paper, pencils.

In the first phase, the youth group is to go to an abortion protest or rally. They are to be observers only. If this option is not possible, invite in people who can objectively express the views of both groups. Allow the kids to ask questions or take notes. This session is to be strictly cerebral.

The second phase takes place at the next session. To begin, break the youths into groups of four and allow them to answer the following questions over a 30 to 45–minute period:

1. What is a good definition for the word *life*?
2. What is a good definition for the word *abortion*?
3. When does life begin? Give a few sentences.
4. When, if ever, should an abortion take place?
5. When, if ever, should Christians justify abortion?
6. Write three questions you want answered by the pro-life and pro-choice factions.

Afterward, have each group give its responses to the questions. Discuss these in detail. Have the kids explain what issues came up during each discussion. Write down all the responses from each question. Tell the young people the questions from number six will be sent to each of the respective parties to await a response. NOTE: If you have a young teen who has experienced an abortion, it might be best if she is briefed on what you are doing ahead of time. Let her observe the discussion on the issue and then, if she desires, tell of her experience and her opinion.

Religious Activities

Christians need good games and activities. City kids often criticize those activities that are religiously oriented, saying they are not relevant to them. It is the purpose of this chapter to create relevant activities that meet urban youths where they are and allow them to come to grips with their concepts of religion, faith, morals, and God.

Religious orientation is essential in the development of urban teens and children. What young people believe about religion can often make a tremendous difference in how they handle themselves when traditional urban problems arise. As drugs, sex, guns, and family degradation (to name just a few) face urban youths, the religions they choose must make a difference in their lives. We must show them that what they are searching for is Jesus.

Christianity is crucial in the city. People have argued that cities are devoid of religion. I beg to differ. The city is full of religion. The question is, "Is the city Christian?" The city has a plethora of religions: Jehovah's Witnesses, Mormons, Nation of Islam, Orthodox Muslims, The Way, and many others—all competing for the young people of urban America. The city is the most religiously saturated place around. There are churches of different types on almost every corner; religion permeates the city. It is a shame that Christianity does not.

As I view the problem of religion versus the presence of Christianity in the city, one thing I notice is that many people accept religions that are not core Christianity under the pretense that they are Christian. In short, people in other religions perceive themselves as serving Christ.

One day I had a discussion with a mother who invited me to her son's baptism. I had been instrumental in her son's understanding of Christianity, but her son consistently rejected it. He had since gone to a juvenile detention school where he accepted Jesus. As the family and I were driving to the baptism, I was amazed at the mother's faith in the salvation of her son. She said often, "I knew he would come to God. I had been praying for him daily. He's saved now. He has Jesus in his heart." After a while, she inquired about the church where I was ministering. I told her and we proceeded to talk for about 15 minutes about Christianity and what it requires of each individual. From the conversation, she seemed very traditional in her views and was extremely sincere. The conversation moved to her, so I asked about the church she attended. To my astonishment she stated, "I'm a member of the Church of Latter-day Saints." I said, "A Mormon?" She affirmed my statement. When I inquired what particularly led her to attend this specific church, she said, "It's a good church. We really study the Bible there. But as far as I'm concerned, it's the only church I know that really preaches Jesus." Christianity is sometimes hampered by other religions that camouflage themselves as Christian.

Urban youths are forced to grow up in an environment where it is confusing to be religious, even more so to be a Christian. Urban church youth groups must be overtly Christian. We must instill within the hearts and minds of our young people the dignity that comes with following Jesus Christ. If you don't do this, many kids can waver in their beliefs when times of Christian testing come. If Christian training and discipleship are not done in some form, you might be setting your young people up for failure in the future.

ALL SAINTS DAY

MATERIALS NEEDED: Poster board, markers.

Instead of focusing on Halloween, focus on "All Saints Day" on November 1. To begin, explain to the children what a saint is. Tell them the Bible describes saints as people whose lives have been consecrated by God through confession of Jesus Christ as Lord. Then explain that God considers all believers part of the community of saints, although Catholic Christians have designated certain special people who have served God and humanity in an extraordinary way to be named saints throughout history.

After this is explained, begin the activity. Look over the following list of saints (official and unofficial) and explain what they have become known for. Then make a list of the children in your program; call it "The Saints of *(your program)*." Ask all of the kids what they would like to be known for. Have them be specific and encourage them to begin now to develop these qualities.

Here are some official and unofficial saints and what they have come to be remembered for.

1. *ST. ANDREW* (the disciple)
   Followed Jesus without hesitation when he called him.
2. *ST. PAUL* (the apostle)
   First great missionary—spreading the Gospel to the Gentiles.
3. *ST. STEPHEN*
   First martyr to Christianity.
4. *MARTIN LUTHER KING, JR.*
   Nonviolent struggle for civil rights.
5. *MOTHER TERESA*
   Cares for the homeless and dying of Calcutta, India.

End the time listing any additional saints the kids think should be listed.

RECOMMENDED
GRADES:
5-7

CHRISTIAN HUNT

**MATERIALS
NEEDED:**
Shopping
center, paper,
pens.

Take your group to a large department store or shopping center. Then form your youths into two or three distinct groups. Each group is to find as many professing Christians as it can in 30 minutes. Each person they find must sign his or her name and denomination. However, the challenge comes when each group must estimate how many people it will find. The group that gets the most people above that number wins. This activity could also be done at an outdoor festival or an airport.

RECOMMENDED
GRADES:
10-12

THE CHURCH'S CREED

**MATERIALS
NEEDED:**
Paper, pens.

This activity is to see how urban youths react when they have to form a church and come up with a statement of faith together. This should be done with groups of ten. The objective is for the kids to pretend they are the founding fathers of a newly formed church. However, they cannot solicit new members until they have drawn up a statement of faith, responded to certain contemporary church issues, and have chosen a pastor from the group. The youth director must express to each group that forming a theological stance is hard. There will be disagreements, but they must be worked out to form a church that everyone is happy with and would be willing to attend. This will happen in three phases.

Phase one: A statement of faith must be written, expressing the theological core of the church. The following must be spelled out in the statement:

1. The church name and denomination
2. The process by which people become Christians

3. The church's stance on life after death
4. The church's stance on baptism and when it is used
5. The role the Holy Spirit plays

Phase two: A statement must be written on what the church believes about the following issues:

1. Can women pastor?
2. Will there be dancing allowed in the church?
3. Is sex allowed before marriage?
4. What will our youth department look like?
5. What will the church do with the funds it collects?
6. What Christian actions should the church take if the pastor becomes corrupt?

Phase three: A pastor must be chosen from the existing group.

Once this has been completed, have each group report what it has decided in each category. Encourage open feedback and ask how easy or strenuous it was to form a church theology. For many, it will have been hard. Explain how this has split and demolished churches. However, it is also what has made many churches great. This activity can have tremendous spiritual repercussions.

THE DEVIL CAN'T WIN

RECOMMENDED GRADES: 5-8

This activity is designed for follow-up discussion. The purpose is to have the group come to a mathematical understanding of why the Devil will be defeated in the end. NOTE: This game is not an attempt at theology, but a demonstrative way to express Isaiah 14. In this chapter, Satan is cast out of heaven with one-third of the heavenly host. Mathematically, that leaves two-thirds that can and will overcome him. This is what is demonstrated.

MATERIALS NEEDED:
None.

This game needs 25 participants divided into three teams. The Devil's team has five players, God's team has ten, and the remaining ten represent the good people. Tell the Devil's team its objective is to destroy the good people by touching them. If they are successful, the good people are out. It is the purpose of God's team to protect the good people from the Devil's team. Last, the Devil's team has seven minutes to complete its mission. Its time is limited in parallel to Christ's second coming. When seven minutes are up, the game is over. Afterward, discuss the results of the game and correlate it with how the Devil attempts to defeat us but God protects us. Although it seems the Devil is sometimes successful, he just doesn't have the manpower to win.

RECOMMENDED
GRADES:
K-4

EVERY LITTLE STEP I TAKE

MATERIALS
NEEDED:
None.

This is recommended to test little children's Scripture memory. Have all the children line up against a wall. The leader then tests them on Scripture they should know. Each child takes a step for each word of the Scripture he or she remembers. The children who travel the farthest distance receive a small reward.

RECOMMENDED
GRADES:
5-8

GOD'S BOX

MATERIALS
NEEDED:
Shoe box,
paper, pencils.

This is a great weekly activity. "God's Box" is a shoe box in which the young people can put questions on pressing issues they want biblical insight on. On a weekly basis, draw two questions and give counsel on them. The questions should be drawn a week in advance, so you can be more thorough in giving scriptural answers. The first week, have the youths sit down and write two questions each to get the box started. This activity is often a great success with youth groups in housing developments, because many of these youths do not attend church and often formulate a street theology to attempt to answer religious questions. This offers them the option of receiving genuine answers.

HALLOWEEN HOUSE

MATERIALS NEEDED:
Available space.

This is a wonderful activity that introduces a Christian theme into Halloween. Similar to a haunted house, the "Halloween House" shows how scary life is without Christ. The theme should display the dichotomy between darkness and light. This is a central theme in Christ's message. There will be no witches and goblins, but the story of Satan and Christ's triumph over him will be explained. The following paragraphs show one way this can be executed.

First, there should be at least four rooms. The theme in room one should be "The Fall of Lucifer." Lucifer, God, and the angels are the characters in this moderately lit room. Explain the arrogance of the most beautiful, who decided he would try to exalt himself higher than God. Show this once wonderful being becoming increasingly evil and the absurdity of this move. End with God casting Lucifer and one-third of the angels out into darkness, where Lucifer takes on a new name—Satan.

Second, room two will be dark (and possibly hot). This is hell. Satan is fiercely angry that he's been thrown into this terrible place. This room should be scary and mean. Here Satan begins to reveal his plan to get back at God by tempting and torturing Christians. A subplot of Job could be done here. End with Satan ordering his demons to harm all Christians.

Room three will contain Christians, angels, demons, and Jesus. In the style of C. S. Lewis' *The Screwtape Letters*, demons constantly attempt to harm the Christians, but the angels don't let them. This room can often be comical. Although the Christians are unaware of the work the angels are doing on their behalf, show the struggle between both forces here. This should all end when Jesus enters and casts the demons away.

In the fourth and final room, Jesus should explain the Christian message as one that brings light into darkness. To get the best effect, slowly light up this room as Jesus speaks until it's fully lit. Here Jesus will explain how we all may be in darkness, but we can enjoy his light if we choose to make him Lord of our lives. The theological stance of your group will determine how evangelistic this final room will be. End with Jesus explaining that he has overcome evil, and then pray.

I'M A PROPHET

MATERIALS NEEDED:
Poster board, markers.

A *prophet* by general definition is anyone who speaks for God. First, explain to the children that God wants all of his people to be prophets for him. That is, he wants us to speak his truth in all situations. Children must understand that any time they stand up for what God tells us is right, they are essentially being prophets to those who are not doing what God says. After each question ask, "How could you be a prophet in this situation?" Second, read the following sample scenarios and responses as a guide for the youths. Since these scenarios are very real, they may be frightening to some children. NOTE: Use this activity with caution and discretion.

1. There are two friends in school; one gets mad and begins to fight with the other. Both of them look to you to be on their side of the fight. How can you be a prophet in this situation? *Response:* "God would not want me to take sides, but to try to break up the fight and help both of you to become friends again."
2. You are outside playing when a drug dealer comes up to you and says, "Here, I'll give you one of these cocaine bags free, if you'll try it." How can you be a prophet in this situation? *Response:* "I would say NO! Jesus hates drugs! And then I would run home and tell my mother or father about this man."
3. You wake from your sleep to hear your mother and father fighting. Your mother is screaming, and you can hear your father

beating her. You get out of bed and begin to walk toward the room. You knock, then enter. Your mother looks really bad. How can you be a prophet in this situation? *Response:* "I would pray and tell them God wants everyone to be good to one another. Then I would ask them to pray and not fight. The next day, I would tell my teacher."

End this exercise by challenging the group to be prophets as serious situations arise. A prophet's message is not necessarily accepted by the hearers, but it must be told.

JEHOVAH'S WITNESS VISITS

RECOMMENDED
GRADES:
8-12

**MATERIALS
NEEDED:**
Outside
speaker.

The purpose of this activity is to give urban youths the opportunity to spread the Gospel. This activity will take five weeks of preparation, one week of evangelism, and two weeks of debriefing. This must happen—being underprepared can be detrimental, even dangerous.

There are two facets to this activity: adult leader training and youth preparation. Adult leaders should learn as much as they can about Jehovah's Witnesses and invite in an outside resource that can help in planning and strategy. Be sure this is thoroughly planned before proceeding.

Once adult leaders have orchestrated their intentions, prepare the youths by studying the following themes:

Week 1: Why do Christians evangelize?
Week 2: What Jehovah's Witnesses believe and what they think of Christians (an outside resource is best).
Week 3: Where Christians believe Jehovah's Witnesses stray, and why Christianity is right (the purpose is strictly apologetic).
Week 4: How should we go about our evangelism? This session should include compiling a list of known Jehovah's Witnesses' homes and meeting sites that your group could visit to

evangelize. It can be as simple as family members, friends, a kingdom hall, or distributing pamphlets.

Week 5: Review, specific planning, and prayer.

Week 6: EVANGELIZE.

Week 7: What have we learned and why is evangelism important to the advancement of the Gospel?

Week 8: The mission is not over—where should we go from here? (You can use this to introduce another religion.)

This activity can be one of the best tools to educate kids on the need for missionaries, or it could be a preactivity before a mission trip. Religions of all types are in the city; our young people must be made aware of them.

RECOMMENDED GRADES:
7-12

"RAP"TURE

MATERIALS NEEDED:
Bibles.

This activity is for those who have creative kids who love to rap. The process is simple. Assign Scripture passages to groups of two to four youths. The objective is to create a rap to the Scripture given. A time limit should be given to finish. When done, each group presents its rap to the others.

This can be an extremely fun time. If the raps are good enough, have the groups present them at a church program, Sunday school, or during church service. I guarantee you they will add a new element to the meaning of scriptural interpretation.

RECOMMENDED GRADES:
10-12

SCRIPTURE PARAPHRASE

Here is something every group should do. It is extremely challenging to the youths, yet it is a scriptural learning experience that often continues to be used when they mature. The purpose of this activity is to challenge youths to translate Scripture passages on their own instead of always depending on others. The process will take instruction, but is easy to do.

To begin, divide youths into teams of four. Each team needs a Bible, a Bible dictionary, a concordance, and a commentary. It is a good aid to have an interlinear Bible or multiple translations available. First, give the youths a Scripture passage to research for a better understanding. Next, teach them how each resource is to be used and unleash them to paraphrase the passage. Last, allow them to explain their paraphrases to you or the other teams. By the time this activity is over, teens are often anxious to paraphrase other passages.

MATERIALS NEEDED: Bibles, Bible dictionaries, concordances, commentaries, paper, pens.

SIN'S POTHOLE

RECOMMENDED GRADES: 8-12

MATERIALS NEEDED: Van.

Pack your group into a van. Your trip should take the group over the roughest road you can think of. Most urban metropolis' have areas of town where potholes are everywhere. Ride for a while until the kids wonder what in the world is going on. Find a place to stop, then ask everyone to get out and look at the rough road.

Begin a discussion on sin. Correlate sin to a pothole. When we do sinful things, it causes bumpy roads for us. Although the sinner might not realize the road is bumpy, those "passengers" who are closest to us will realize things are not natural about the road we are traveling. Then the youth leader must ask, "What could one do to make this road smooth again?" Many will suggest filling the holes to make the road smooth again, but you should disagree. As most cities have found, filling potholes does not solve the problem. The pothole will only pop up again in a few months. The only way to smooth out a street with potholes is to repair the entire street—to dig up the worn tar and lay fresh tar. Many people are convinced that if they consciously make themselves aware of their sins, this will cure their sins. But it will not—sin will only return. It is our responsibility to ask Jesus to hew out our sinful lifestyles and lay a new coating filled with his blessing.

<table>
<tr><td>

RECOMMENDED
GRADES:
5-12

</td><td>

STEEL MOUNTAIN DEVOTIONS

</td></tr>
</table>

**MATERIALS
NEEDED:**
Large bridge.

This is an interesting way to have a devotional in the city. Reading the Bible is often difficult for urban young people because many of the images used are not images common to their situations. This activity is great when explaining the Exodus story. Take a small group of youths to a big bridge (if possible, one that overlooks a vast area). At the bottom of the bridge, begin to explain the story of Moses and how Mount Zion was where he went to meet God himself. As you walk up the bridge, begin to explain how Mount Zion was frightening to the Israelites. When you reach the apex of the bridge, have everyone look around and take in the sight. Begin to explain the story of the Ten Commandments and correlate this bridge-top experience with Moses' mountaintop experience. As you descend the bridge, mention how Moses aged because of his time with God and the Israelites' unfaithfulness to God. This is a practical method to relate biblical topics and urban experience.

<table>
<tr><td>

RECOMMENDED
GRADES:
1-4

</td><td>

WHAT WOULD GOD OR THE DEVIL SAY?

</td></tr>
</table>

**MATERIALS
NEEDED:**
None.

This activity is a discussion starter for little kids about how God and the Devil react in certain situations. It is often a help to children to be able to view God and the Devil in relation to life situations. Therefore, this activity takes the form of three scenarios.

1. You find $500 in an envelope on your way home from school. It has the name of one of your neighbors on it. (Maybe you could get an envelope and put a fictitious person's name on it. Inside place a few dollar bills—just to make more of an impact with the story.) You decide to take some of it and buy a gold ring, new sneakers, and a new coat before returning the rest. When you

return it, you say, "This was all that was in the envelope." What would the Devil say? What would God say?

2. You are in the local candy store. (Ask the kids the name of such a store if you do not know it and use it in the story.) You see one of your friends take three packs of candy off the rack. Your friend then gives you one when the store owner's back is turned. You quickly walk out of the store laughing, happy that you got a free pack of candy. What would the Devil say? What would God say?

3. The kid who always makes fun of you for the way you dress is tripped on the way to recess and rips his pants. You laugh and tease him in front of the whole school. What would the Devil say? What would God say?

Close the session by asking the kids to pray that God will allow them to do things his way instead of the Devil's way.

WRITE A SERMON

RECOMMENDED GRADES:
7-12

MATERIALS NEEDED: Writing paper or tape recorder, Bible, take-home assignments.

Sermon writing is often viewed as something that should only be done by the minister. This activity allows young people to expound the Word of God on a specific topic and present it to the group. Near the end of your group time, announce you need three people who are willing to write or record a sermon. They will each work with the same topic. Before these volunteers leave, tell them each sermon needs to be five to ten minutes in length. If they don't want to read their sermons before the group, they can prepare them on tape to be played to the others. Next, when it comes time to present each sermon, listen to them consecutively. Finally, have the group discuss similarities and differences between the sermons. Use this activity to bring home the message that although the Scriptures have one central theme, they are often interpreted in different ways.

RECOMMENDED GRADES: 8-12

MATERIALS NEEDED:
Poster board, markers, paper, pens.

A YOUTH LIBERATION FOR YOUR CHURCH

Often the church can become old, rigid, and even stagnant. This activity gives the young people a chance to make suggestions that would make things more exciting for them within the church body. Explain that young people occasionally need to remind their elders what is really important. The same must periodically happen in the church. Tell the group the resolutions from this discussion will be given directly to the pastor as a youth group suggestion. Cover issues like church worship, Sunday school, catechism, church staff availability, even ask questions pertaining to the effectiveness of the youth group. Keep the discussion upbeat and maintain a positive atmosphere. Do not consistently dwell on the negatives, but incorporate discussion on those things that are going well. Finally, have the youths discuss what they are willing to do for the church to make the items in the proposal come true. Afterward, write a proposal to the pastor incorporating all the facets discussed. Have the kids give it the final approval before sending it.

This activity allows the youths to find a constructive means to revitalize the church. Most pastors take kindly to such a gesture. It is also a way to let the church know the youth group wants to be a vital element in the church.

Cultural Activities

12

CHAPTER

Cultural activities serve two purposes. First, they attempt to create a sense of identity within an individual. This identity arises from realizing the cultural value and beauty of one's own particular race. To get children to proudly identify with their race is to get them to identify with what is most culturally beautiful about themselves. Second, cultural activities create esteem. The struggle of urban youth ministry is to convince city kids who have constantly been rejected that they are *special*—prized possessions created in God's image. Esteem is often low among urban youths. Ironically, the pride that does exist is often buffoonish—a facade to impress or seem tough. When young people are allowed to see themselves from a cultural point of view, they will see a heritage, a richness, and a depth that will mirror esteem to them.

It is a deep concern of mine that urban youths don't know much about themselves culturally and are rarely challenged to learn creatively about their culture. Culture is extremely important; it is the vital core of an individual. When people understand that they have an ancient heritage and culture, they begin to have a balanced sense of self that enhances both themselves and their race. It has been a concern of educators and youth workers that city children have no concept of who they are and who they can become. I suggest that culture is one element in identity formation. We lose something valuable in people if we don't allow them to see themselves as beautiful.

I was once quizzing a group of 13 African-American eighth and ninth graders about great heroic figures in their culture. What I found was startling. I began by asking, "Who was Harriet Tubman?" They hesitated, then one boy responded, "I know she was a conductor." I was puzzled at the response, so I asked him what he meant. He clarified by stating, "She was a conductor of a railroad of trains." No one argued with him because they did not realize Harriet Tubman was a participant in freeing slaves through a movement called the "Underground Railroad." This has nothing to do with a train operation.

I dismissed this occurrence as chance and proceeded to ask another question. "Who was Frederick Douglass?" I received no intelligent response. This confused me a bit because I assumed eighth and ninth graders should know this. I continued by asking, "Can anyone tell me who invented peanut butter?" The feedback was similar to the previous responses.

By this time, I had had enough. I decided I would ask an easier question, one they *had* to know. I said, "Someone tell me something about Martin Luther King, Jr." The two responses I received were: "Wasn't he the man who went to sleep and had a dream?" and "He was shot because he was nice."

At this point, I was mentally ready to switch gears. I decided to use this exercise to show the youths how little knowledge they possessed about themselves. I asked, "Who was George Washington?" As I expected, every hand went up. Most said, "He was the first president." Others stated, "He never told a lie." I then asked, "Does anyone know what Betsy Ross did?" Most affirmed she was known for making flags during the colonial period. Only two kids didn't know who she was. I moved on to ask, "Who was Abraham Lincoln?" The dialogue really began then. In detail, this group expressed that Abraham Lincoln was not only the sixteenth president, but one youth yelled, "He freed the slaves by signing the Emancipation Proclamation in 1863!" I must admit, this blew me away.

I then posed another question to them, "Why is it that we know so much about this history and know so little about the other?" They honestly didn't know. Nor did they understand why they didn't know anything about African-American history, until one 14-year-old girl said, "Well, Nelson, I guess the reason we don't know our history is because we never learned it." Precisely.

Urban minority young people are culturally crippled whenever the historical basics of their own people are disregarded for the history of the larger society. A people without a history is a people who will have no future. Therefore, those of us entrusted with the responsibility of doing urban ministry must create games and activities for young people that enhance cultural consciousness.

The activities in this chapter are weighted toward African-American youth; however, they are broad enough to be adapted by all cultures.

ART IN MUSIC

RECOMMENDED
GRADES:
3-6

Art is often a passageway to creativity. This activity allows youths to begin to appreciate art by identifying it with themselves and their favorite music covers.

First, the youth leader must ask the kids beforehand to bring favorite records from home that have some form of art distinctive to their culture on the covers. When the kids arrive, place all the albums in one place. You will use these for object lessons. Also, have paintings or photos of art from African, Hispanic, Asian, and other cultures displayed. Have the group look at them as you explain the basics of cultural artistic expression. You should point out such things as facial features, body spacing, foreground, and background. Next, return the albums to the children. This time have them point out to you the features on the album covers that exemplify distinct

MATERIALS NEEDED:
Photographs or paintings, watercolors, white construction paper, brushes.

175

cultural artistic understanding. Last, have the kids paint their own pictures, expressing their views of their culture's art.

BIG . . .

MATERIALS NEEDED:
A large banner sheet, markers.

This activity is to educate young people about their homelands—big China, big Australia, big Mexico, big Africa, or whatever nationality the kids come out of. Many are from families that are second and third generations away from the homeland. The older adults will often speak of their places of national origin, but many of the children disregard this heritage because they have never actually known this place as home.

In this activity, the members of a group work on a big map of their homeland. This map must be as extensive as possible. All cities, mountain ranges, bodies of water, and countries within that homeland should be labeled. Once the entire map is completed, it looks best if colored. If you desire, spend a couple of weeks studying the history behind certain cities and the cultures that have arisen from them. Have the kids identify and mark areas where known relatives are from. Most of all, teach the youths to be proud of this land. This is their historical past and the place where their culture shines brightest.

FASHION EXTRAVAGANZA

MATERIALS NEEDED:
Clothing.

This is a great idea for an urban youth pastor who wants to have a fund-raiser with the youth group. Have a "Fashion Extravaganza" night. This will be an evening of cultural fashion, elegance, and variety in which the youths strut their stuff for the audience. Have young people bring clothing from their own collection. Make this evening humorous by renaming some of the kids or some of the clothing. Make it seem as if they are professional models who have traveled the world. What makes this evening is having different categories of clothing (for instance, cultural garb, sportswear, school clothing, church wear, business attire). NOTE: If planned far enough in advance, you can often get genuine, elegant, and professional clothing donated for the evening from clothing stores.

I AM LIKE . . .

RECOMMENDED GRADES: **4-7**

MATERIALS NEEDED: Newsprint, markers, newspaper, encyclopedias, and other reference resources.

Here is a cultural comparison activity that has been successful in having young people identify themselves with a great person from their culture. To begin, make a list of great cultural heroes of the culture from which the youths come. This listing should have a variety of personalities within that culture—entertainers, scientists, musicians, authors, freedom fighters, and educators. Articles, encyclopedias, or reference resources should be made available for the youths to look up each personality to determine which people they'd most like to emulate. Each young person will report to the group what drew him or her to the personality chosen. This is a good activity for a small group that is geared to cultural academics or as an option to learn more about cultural role models.

IDENTIFYING *KWANZAA*

RECOMMENDED GRADES: **2-6**

MATERIALS NEEDED: Index cards.

Kwanzaa is an African-American holiday and lifestyle wherein there are seven principles that if practiced can encourage unity within the race. There must be an instruction on the principles of *Kwanzaa* before this activity takes place. The principles are sevenfold.

1. *Umoja* (unity)
2. *Kujichagulia* (self-determination)
3. *Ujima* (collective work and responsibility)
4. *Ujamaa* (cooperative economics)

177

5. *Nia* (purpose)
6. *Kuumba* (creativity)
7. *Imani* (faith)

The goal of this learning game is to identify Swahili *Kwanzaa* terms that are flashed amidst made-up words. The kid who identifies the *Kwanzaa* term must then give the English meaning of the word.

One card will be flashed to one child at a time. If the first card is *Kullazig*, the child has two response options. He or she can either identify it as a *Kwanzaa* term or reject it as a fake. In this case, it's a made-up word. If the card happens to be a *Kwanzaa* term and the child identifies it as such, she or he must then give its English translation in order to get credit.

RECOMMENDED GRADES:
8-12

IT'S A CULTURAL THING YOU WOULDN'T UNDERSTAND

MATERIALS NEEDED:
Writing paper, poster board, markers, pencils.

This activity is dedicated to helping youths understand more fully what makes their culture unique. Within every cultural group, there are behaviors that are a part of the heritage of the people. These behaviors are often misunderstood by other cultural groups. Uniqueness is often translated in negative terms. This activity translates it into esteem.

First, divide the group into teams of four. Second, provide each team with three sheets of poster board and a marker. Third, have the kids respond to each question below on the three separate sheets of paper. The questions are as follows:

1. Name as many things as you can that are unique to your culture but that are often misunderstood by others.
2. Name some things about other cultures that seem different to you.
3. Is it possible for a person of one culture to fully understand what it is like to be a part of another culture? Why or why not?

Afterward, post each sheet up front. Discuss in detail what the youths believe on these issues. Allow them to understand the uniqueness of their culture and appreciate it. End by emphasizing that there is a uniqueness within all cultural groups. This is not a negative aspect, but should be viewed as positive.

JESUS IS LIKE ME

RECOMMENDED GRADES: **8-12**

MATERIALS NEEDED: Newsprint, markers.

Contemporary Christianity has not often portrayed Jesus as one who loves the culture of minorities. Thereby, many urban youths reject Jesus simply because he is characterized as "the white man's God." This activity helps urban youths realize that Jesus also favors them and their culture.

First, ask the kids what they see as most beautiful and unique about their culture. List these things and discuss why they believe this is so. Second, have the youths list what they believe are the most beautiful and unique things about Jesus. Discuss these characteristics. Third, ask what Jesus' beauty and their cultural characteristics have in common. Have them come up with the answers. Last, close the discussion and make your point that Jesus is the pinnacle of culture. He loves that which is best in all cultures and is an active part of the culture from which they come.

KNOW THYSELF

RECOMMENDED GRADES: **8-12**

MATERIALS NEEDED: Newsprint, markers.

This is a cultural game show. The team to gain the most points in 30 minutes wins. Each team must answer questions that should be common knowledge to its culture or race.

To begin, a staff member should be chosen as the game show leader. Next, there should be two teams of five people each. Each team chooses a question from one of the three posted categories: people, events, or places. All questions are to be culturally centered. Each group chooses a team spokesperson who will state the group's answer. After each question is asked, the group is given ten seconds to give its answer. If the first group misses, the question is passed to the other team to attempt to answer. Once the half hour has expired, if the teams are close enough to risk points, they are to wager a certain amount of points on one final question to determine the winner.

<table><tr><td>**RECOMMENDED GRADES:**
1-4</td></tr></table>

KWANZAA SCRAMBLE

MATERIALS NEEDED:
Construction paper.

Like an earlier activity, this is a great learning game concerning *Kwanzaa*. To begin, divide the kids into two teams. The purpose is to have one team unscramble the seven principles of *Kwanzaa* before the challenging team can.

Consequently, there must be an instruction on the principles of *Kwanzaa* before this activity takes place. The principles are sevenfold.

1. *Umoja* (unity)
2. *Kujichagulia* (self-determination)
3. *Ujima* (collective work and responsibility)
4. *Ujamaa* (cooperative economics)
5. *Nia* (purpose)
6. *Kuumba* (creativity)
7. *Imani* (faith)

NOTE: This activity can be used for any group of kids during the *Kwanzaa* season (December 26 through January 1).

<table><tr><td>**RECOMMENDED GRADES:**
9-12</td></tr></table>

MALE RESPONSIBILITY TEST

The city is often a place of male abandonment. Often the finger is pointed to the failure of men to live up to their responsibilities. Thus, cultural and family discord results. This activity is geared to the boys and can be executed in one of two ways. The first way is to write the following questions on paper and have the young men respond. The second way is to discuss each of these questions as a group. Before giving these questions, educate your young men on the tragedy of urban male irresponsibility regarding both their culture and their women. The questions to help understand male cultural responsibility are as follows:

MATERIALS NEEDED: Paper.

1. What ideal characteristics would a responsible male of your culture have?
2. How true is it when people say urban males are not responsible to their culture and women?
3. Are you a responsible male? What makes you think so?
4. Do you have any cultural male role models? Why did you pick them?
5. Why do you think many of our males falter in their responsibilities to women, especially when a baby is born?
6. How important is it to live a life free of drugs and alcohol?
7. Is it important for a responsible male to be religious? Why or why not?
8. What is your educational goal, and why is it important to your liberation?
9. If you could be a role model to any three young men, who would they be? What would you teach them?
10. Is it bad if a man cries?
11. Why is it important for males to be sensitive to women?
12. Describe the type of woman you wish to marry one day.
13. Does the race of this woman matter to you? Give a reason for your answer.
14. Is sex all there is to being a man?
15. Can a man be fulfilled without sexual activity?
16. If you ever found out your girlfriend was pregnant (and the baby was yours), what would you do?

17. In three words, describe your father.
18. In three words, describe how you want to be known as a father.
19. Name three areas you must become more responsible in. Why?
20. When you raise your children, what things do you most desire to teach them?
21. When you raise your children, how important will Christianity be to your family?
22. If you had to choose one man from our culture to be an example to all our men, who would he be?

Afterward, respond to each question in an understanding manner. Help the young men process what they are articulating, and above all, make them understand the full implications of their statements. Be ready for heated discussion. This is healthy. Before ending, be sure each teen understands the importance of being a responsible man, dedicated to both his culture and his woman.

RECOMMENDED GRADES:
8-12

MARTIN/MALCOLM DEBATE

MATERIALS NEEDED:
Poster board, paper, pencils, markers.

Martin Luther King, Jr. and Malcolm X are the foremost civil rights influences among the African-American youth culture. The debate of the day is which one's philosophical stance is capable of directing the urban underclass. This activity is geared to make urban youths come to an opinion about which man they believe to be closest to the truth, if either.

First, someone has to impartially explain to the youths both philosophies and the views of these men on the liberation of the African-American underclass. If you feel inadequate to do so, bring in an outside resource. This should take no longer than ten minutes. Second, post around the room three signs marked Martin, Malcolm, and Neither. Have each youth stand under the sign he or she believes in. Let each group know it has now entered a debate. The youths will have ten minutes to construct a defense for their stances. When the deadline is up, allow a time for response and rebuttal. Last, thank the group for tough-mindedly and intelligently tackling this issue. Close with your opinions and views on this topic.

MUSIC OF MY CULTURE

RECOMMENDED
GRADES:
8-12

**MATERIALS
NEEDED:**
Paper, pencils.

To begin this game, a large multicultural group is needed. The group must first be split into cultural segments (for example, Hispanic, Asian, European-American, African-American). Once the groups are formed, each group must be given a few lines of poetry from the same poem. Give each group ten minutes to create a song out of the poetry it was given. Anything the kids need must exist naturally; no audio equipment will be given. When time expires, have each group present its song to the others. This is often the funniest part of the whole activity. What will easily be noticed is that each ethnic group will create a song that sounds typical of the culture from which it comes. Finally, begin to discuss how cultural differences can be a beautifying factor instead of a negative factor. Cultural differences are to be complementary, not contradictory. The beauty of these songs is not the words of the poem, but the cultural translations of the poem.

MY COMPLEXION, YOUR COMPLEXION

RECOMMENDED
GRADES:
2-4

**MATERIALS
NEEDED:**
Colored paper.

Within many minority cultures, there is a tacit dilemma concerning skin shade. Those who have lighter skin tones often tease those who have darker tones. Those who have lighter tones consider their complexions closer to the predominant society and, therefore, have a feeling they are somehow better. As a result, they look on those of their own culture who are darker as being inferior. This mind-set is still prevalent. The following activity attempts to correct this.

To begin, seat your group in a circle. Display as many colorings of the youths' culture as possible. As the children are observing the colors, ask them if they know people who have complexions like the colors they are viewing. Then ask them to point to the colors closest to their own complexions. Ask, "If you had the choice of being any complexion that you see displayed, which would it be?" What commonly occurs is that those who are lighter tend to choose the same complexion, but those who are dark choose a lighter shade. Finally, inform the group of the following important facets:

1. Be proud of your complexion; your best identity will come from those of your same complexion (race)
2. Skin color is given from God
3. It cannot be changed
4. It's not the complexions of people that make up who and what they are, but who they are inside

This can be a challenging concept to little children who have been societally and culturally influenced that the lighter complexion is the better one.

MY HAIR, YOUR HAIR

MATERIALS NEEDED: Baby dolls, cardboard.

This is similar to the previous activity. Like the complexion, the length and texture of one's hair has an extreme influence on one's personal outlook. Among many minority groups, people are trying everything on the market to get their hair to be long and soft, even if this is against the natural look and texture of their hair. In short, hair is often classified by minority groups as "good" or "bad." Bad hair is often defined as "nappy," "greasy," and "kinky," even if these are natural inclinations of that culture's hairstyle. On the other hand, good hair is defined as having the style and length of normal European hairstyles.

To begin, display two baby dolls in the front of the room. One must have long hair, the other must be similar to the natural complexion of the culture. Be sure the dolls are of the same color. Next, hold up two cardboard signs. One will say "Good Hair," the other "Bad Hair." Tell the kids they must place one sign at each doll, by general vote. Inquire why they placed the signs where they did. Usually, if the group is culturally esteemed, it will pick the doll whose hair is closest to the kids' culture no matter how badly the hair has been presented. As your closing, adapt the four points from the last activity.

OUR NEIGHBORHOOD HEROES

RECOMMENDED GRADES:
5-12

MATERIALS NEEDED: Poster board, markers, paper, pencils.

In most urban communities, there are many unsung heroes who are often overlooked. Ordinary people who are pivotal to the community's development are often dismissed as "just doing their jobs." On many cultural days, the people who are idolized are either dead or the kids don't know them personally. In short, what is communicated to the kids is that those who are famous within the race cannot and could not arise from their community.

Have the group come up with a list of people who are heroes in the community. The list usually includes resident leaders, custodial staff, active mothers and fathers, management leaders, and youth leaders. Make a big card that says, "Our Neighborhood Heroes." Have the group visit each person listed, request the hero to sign the card, and ask the hero for details on how she or he got started.

RACIAL UNDERSTANDING CLUB

RECOMMENDED GRADES:
8-12

MATERIALS NEEDED: None.

Here is an excellent urban activity for groups of two differing cultures. The great thing about any city is there is often a plethora of cultures within its walls. This activity gets two or more different youth groups together, to become better acquainted. During this time, at least the following three things should be discussed:

1. What is it that is unique about each of our cultures?
2. Do our cultures have bad feelings toward each other? If so, why?
3. What can we consistently do to set an example for this city?

These questions often bring up other constructive issues; follow them through. Afterward, have the youths share in a snack with one another. This activity can have long-term effects on how your youths observe differing parts of the city and can often facilitate good friendships.

RECOMMENDED GRADES: 8-12

WHAT'S IN A NAME?

MATERIALS NEEDED:
Paper ballots, pens.

Most cultural groups in America debate which formal name the ethnic group should be called (for example, *Asian* or *Oriental*; *Hispanic* or *Latino*; *Indian* or *Native-American*; *black* or *African-American*). This activity will involve a persuasive vote. For simplicity, the terms *black* and *African-American* will be used.

Tell the group members they are the only ones who can decide the direction of this issue. Proceed to impartially explain the dilemma between the use of *black* and *African-American*. Tell them they must take a vote on which term should be used. Make this announcement sound urgent. Before the vote, tell the youths this is such a crucial issue that a few people will be allowed to come forward and persuasively lobby the group to vote his or her way. This can take a while, so give it the time it needs. When the discussion is completed, take a vote. Count up the ballots and announce which term won approval. Feel free to conclude by sharing your own opinions on the issue.

Environmental Activities

It is the goal of the environmental activities in this chapter to help urban young people struggle with those ecological issues that face urban America, the nation, and the world. The world in which many urban youths live can be considered a microcosm of global deterioration. The testing ground for many of these games and activities can be wrought directly from the city. The contemporary urban metropolis has within it enough environmental maladies to offer a great place to educate city kids on this issue.

As I consider urban environmental problems, they are mostly problems that arise out of excessive wants. The city becomes a never-ending consumption machine in which the primary function is to satisfy its wants over its needs. As a result, the city becomes an insatiable beast that cannot be tamed enough to consider that its destruction is a result of its consumption. As I visit various cities, it amazes me how I can always tell when I'm approaching an urban area. Trash and air pollution are usually my cues.

One day I was driving through the Mojave Desert approaching the greater Los Angeles area. As I drew closer, the environment changed dramatically. My drive went from a crisp blue, clear sky to a grayish brown sky; from an unlittered environment, to one with a lot of trash. The air quality was different. In the desert, I could honestly take in a breath of fresh air; not so in the city. The smog was ever present. You could see and smell the pollution. These changes all happened within a 40-mile radius.

Interestingly, this can be said for almost every large metropolis. The city is an environmental creature that lives, breathes, consumes, and affects those within its borders. To believe anything other is naive. Kids must realize they have a responsibility to influence their environment to the good. This must be emphasized with urban young people.

I was directing a summer camp in a Philadelphia low-cost housing development when I got my staff together to decide how to give a positive message to the kids about the trash problem in their neighborhood. We decided we would have a trash party. We broke all of the age groups into teams and gave them particular sections of the housing development to clean. This was not just a clean-up-and-go operation, however. It was a race between the groups to see how much trash each group could collect in one hour. The group with the most filled trash bags was to get a special prize during the trash party. Within that hour, the youths of that neighborhood collected 102 bags of trash. The 50 bags I bought were gone after the first 20 minutes. The housing project's janitorial staff, seeing what the kids were doing, gave us the remaining bags free. When it was all over, we had a big celebration—it was a great day. The results were incredible: The same young people who had thrown trash on the ground earlier that day refused to let anyone throw trash anywhere but into a trash can.

We must create games and activities that will bring this type of awareness to life for them. Activities that were created and executed with the purpose of restoring nature back to its original state will be found in this chapter. The city is a major factor in the ecological salvation of our planet. If urban young people begin to do what they can to save the environment today, it will instill a desire to continue to take care of it tomorrow.

BIG GROUP RECYCLING CHALLENGE

RECOMMENDED GRADES: All

MATERIALS NEEDED: Recycling bins.

This is a fun activity made for different city groups to challenge one another. Although it doesn't matter how many groups there are, the purpose is to involve as many city youth groups as possible in a recycling challenge.

First, have each participating group commit to this project for one school year. Second, each group should have recycling bins for tin, aluminum, glass, paper, and plastic. These will be the five challenge categories. The youth group that collects the most in each category will receive a prize. Make the prizes big. However, every participating group should be commended in some fashion. A big award banquet for all groups is a wonderful way to show them appreciation.

BUILD A TRASH BOX

RECOMMENDED GRADES: 7-12

MATERIALS NEEDED: Large boxes, trash bags, paper, poster board, tape, colored markers.

This activity is geared to clean up your community and promote your youth group at the same time. Trash often exists because there are not enough places to put it, not because people want a dirty community.

This activity is a cheap remedy to the problem. Before the next youth group meeting, go out to supermarkets or warehouses and ask for large boxes. Predetermine how many trash boxes you want to make. Get a variety of sizes. Next, when the young people arrive, place them in groups around the boxes. Explain to them the importance of having a clean community and how trash can often affect how people view themselves. Convince them that this is no way for people to live, and they can make a difference today!

Each team will have 15 minutes to make its box suitable for a trash box. The kids will color and decorate it, then write "Trash Box" on it in large letters. On another part of the box, it should be noted that this trash can was made courtesy of the youth group. The trash box should overtly promote your youth group. When finished, have the groups put the trash boxes in hallways and corridors around the community and in places strategic to trash collection. While the youths begin to have a sense of invested interest in the beautification of their community, the trash boxes will be spreading the message that your youth group exists for the community. If you choose to do this activity, you must also commit to changing the trash boxes when full. NOTE: In some urban housing developments, the management office must approve this activity first.

RECOMMENDED GRADES:
5-12

ENDANGERED SPECIES GAME

MATERIALS NEEDED:
Smocks or rags, photos of endangered species.

This activity can help start a discussion about endangered species. Before this activity begins, explain to your group what an endangered species is and why it is important to understand the consequences of hunting these animals. Give a few examples such as the California condor, the thick-billed parrot, the snow leopard, the Bengal tiger, and the peregrine falcon. After you establish conceptually what an endangered species is, begin the game.

This activity works best outdoors with a group of ten to 15 players. To begin, choose a team of four to be the endangered species. Give these kids bright smocks to wear or have them tie on rags for identification. Tell the endangered species team its objective is to keep the smocks or rags on or they will be out. Everyone else will be hunters. The objective of the hunters is to gather the last four of the endangered species by removing their smocks or rags. When they have disabled the four players, the species will be extinct. Stake out a play area where the game is to take place (a football field is preferable). The game should last no more than eight minutes.

When the game is over, sit everyone down and have the endangered team members express the feelings they experienced as they attempted to survive. Most will say they thought it unfair or that it was a setup; there was no way they could have won. Take what they say and incorporate it into a discussion on how an endangered species is fighting a losing battle, considering the options that are facing these animals. It is best to be visual with this activity. Present photographs of endangered and extinct animals. Have your group discuss what can be done to help these animals live. Incite them to action of some type, whether it is writing a letter to a congressman, having an animal expert come in to talk, or going to a wildlife refuge. This is an object lesson that urban young people need to be confronted with.

ENVIRONMENTAL MURAL

RECOMMENDED GRADES:
5-12

MATERIALS NEEDED:
Paper, pencils, coloring markers, paint.

This activity involves a craft and the actual construction of a mural. To begin the craft, hand out sheets of folded white paper and have the young people write on one half "A World People CARE About." On the other half, have them write "A World People DON'T CARE About." Next, have them each draw a picture corresponding with

A World People CARE About.

A World People DON'T CARE About.

each phrase. Influence them to draw environmental scenes from either their neighborhood or the city.

Once all have finished drawing, have the group vote upon which one should be made into a wall mural to place in the community. When this has been decided, shape up the picture a bit if necessary. Finally, spend a few days as a group transferring this drawing from the paper to a wall. Your group will be proud of this mural when done.

ENVIRONMENTAL STUDY

MATERIALS NEEDED:
Thermometer, trash bags, notepads.

This long-term activity works best if there is a wooded area nearby. It will show urban kids the ecological changes that can take place in their own neighborhood in one year. First, head out into the woods and stake out an area the group wants to see develop over a year (approximately an acre or less). Pick a diverse area with trees or a stream. Second, the group must make a pact to visit once a month to record changes in the area. Keep a record of at least the following:

1. Temperature
2. Season
3. Is there any new growth? Why?
4. Has anything died or deteriorated? Why?
5. Does anything live here other than plants? Look for holes. See if anything lives under any rocks.
6. Is there any unnatural material? If trash is found, remove it.

Once the group has recorded information, get the kids together to openly decipher what, if anything, is changing in this plot. If changes are normal, ask the group how it can encourage normal growth. If changes are not normal, ask the group what can be done to stabilize the area. Last, keep records and compare them monthly. Allow the young people to really get into this activity. This can be a visual tool to give young people a chance to view their community as ecological scientists. This activity can allow you a springboard for environmental spinoffs.

FIELD CLEANUP

RECOMMENDED GRADES: 5-12

This is a great way for a youth group to provide a recreation area for itself. If you have an abandoned lot that is weeded over but would provide great recreation space, clean it up. A safe field cleanup should take place in these stages.

MATERIALS NEEDED: Lawn mower, trash bags, weed cutter, rakes, gloves, dust masks.

Stage one: Weed Attack
The group will be armed with gloves, dust masks, and trash bags. They will enter the lot and uproot all weeds over one foot.
Stage two: Trash Attack
The group will collect noticeable trash and glass articles and put them in trash bags. Consider recycling the contents.
Stage three: Stake Your Ground
The leader should use the lawn mower to cut the rest of the field. No young people are to be on the lot at this time. If the ground was not cleared thoroughly, a rock or piece of glass could hit someone.
Stage four: Make It Your Own

The group will rake and bag the remains and make the field fit the group's needs and visions.

GARDEN PLANTING

RECOMMENDED GRADES: 2-7

This activity allows urban young people to understand how planting a garden and taking care of it can reap social benefits. This should be delivered as a presentation.
First, you should bring in some pretty garden plants to display for

MATERIALS NEEDED: Plants, shovel.

the kids. Begin with this question, "Why is it important to plant a garden?" Most children will indicate it is because gardens are pretty and smell good. Affirm positive statements about gardens.

Then ask, "What is different about the yards in the neighborhood that have gardens compared to those that don't?" Expect responses about there being less trash and weeds in gardened yards or that these people take pride in their property.

Next ask, "Which home do you think drug dealers would stand in front of?" Most should respond the one without botanical beauty. Then ask, "Which yard would drug dealers be more likely to want to throw trash into?" The response should be the same.

Finally, take the entire group out into the neighborhood and plant the displayed flowers in a secure part of the neighborhood. Care for them until they are acclimated to the soil.

RECOMMENDED GRADES: 2-4

I CAN

MATERIALS NEEDED: None.

This activity allows children to become aware of what they can do to make their neighborhood a better place. First, tell every youth the community cannot survive without her or his support. You are looking for people who are willing to be heroes. However, these heroes must be willing to help out anywhere and anytime to make their neighborhood a better place.

Second, walk the group around the entire neighborhood. Before you go, explain that the only way they can communicate is by starting a sentence with, "I can. . . ." When youths begin this statement, they will end it with something they can do to help the community. You will hear such things as, "I can erase wall writing." "I can pick up bottles." "I can throw away that trash." Afterward, decide when you can return to act on some of these suggestions.

RECOMMENDED
GRADES:
K-4

MUD POTTERY

The objective here is to make pots out of mud. This is a fun and messy craft. Think of this activity as making fudge. First, you need to mix ground dirt and water until the consistency is in favor of dirt. The lump should be moldable, but not too watery. You may need to add water periodically to avoid premature drying. Second, mold the mud into a pot shape that satisfies the group. Allow it to dry thoroughly. Be careful when handling; often mud can be brittle. Third, if the pot feels strong enough, fill it with dirt and begin to use it for a temporary pot. Most pots don't last long, but they offer an inexpensive craft option.

**MATERIALS
NEEDED:**
Water, dirt.

RECOMMENDED
GRADES:
5-12

NOISE POLLUTION SOLUTION

Before kids come into the youth group, get a boom box and blast it. It should be nearly deafening. As young people come in, welcome them as normal. If they ask about the music, tell them it's an informal party. Expect some of them to enter dancing. It is your objective to see if the group will ever think the music is too loud. If it seems the group doesn't care about the noise level, then bring out a second boom box and blast a different song. This will cause enough listening confusion that the group will ask for one of them to be turned off. Once you reach the point where the group thinks the music is either too loud or confusing, turn the music off and have the youths take seats.

Next ask, "Why did you ask me to turn the music off?" Sound upset, then solicit responses. Play devil's advocate for a while with such responses as, "It didn't sound too loud to me." or "What's wrong with you, can't you listen to two things at once?" Once you have the group in an uproar, change the mood and inform them of

**MATERIALS
NEEDED:**
Boom box.

the effects of the noise pollution they inflict on themselves. Many urban youths listen to music constantly. It becomes their existence. The volumes at which they listen to music is a contributing factor to the deafening of youths. We live in an age of Walkman radios that influence the inner ear at a distance of less than an inch. Impress this upon them and encourage the kids to turn down the noise.

RECOMMENDED GRADES:
K-6

PLANTING IN FAITH

MATERIALS NEEDED: Construction paper, markers, scissors, glue, tulip bulbs, shovel.

This activity will make children aware that faith is a necessary element when planting flowers. This activity has two parts and should be done during the fall. Part one involves a craft. The purpose of the craft is to illustrate the growth of tulip bulbs to a flowering state.

to be sure of things we hope for...

FAITH

to be convinced of things we cannot see. Hebrews 11:1

Before you begin, discuss the word *faith*. Use Hebrews 11:1 as your key text. First, preprint the verse on white construction paper (or any light color). Second, cut four bulb shapes, one sprout shape, two leaf shapes, and one complete tulip shape with two full leaves. Third, have the kids glue in succession four growth processes. Start with the single bulb, then the sprout, then two leaves, and finally the full tulip. Have the kids write the word *faith* across their papers. Correlate the verse with this activity by expressing that it takes faith to trust that God will bring about growth.

Part two is practical. After finishing the craft, take the children outside to plant real tulip bulbs. Have a small ceremony (including a prayer and a song), reminding the children if they continue to have faith, they will see tulips in the spring.

RECYCLING CAMPAIGN

RECOMMENDED GRADES:
All

MATERIALS NEEDED:
Trash cans.

This activity needs to be done more often in the city. It is very easy to do. Many of the items and articles used in cities are discarded for waste. Items like glass, aluminum, paper, and some plastics can be reused again if we take seriously the duty of recycling. You must first have a trash can for each item you intend to collect. These trash cans must be displayed. At every group meeting, young people should bring something they collected for recycling. Allow the collected items to accumulate until there is enough to sell. Throw a celebration or plan a trip with the money.

SPLASH OR TRASH

RECOMMENDED GRADES:
7-12

This is a fun race that encourages trash cleanup. To begin, split the group into pairs and give four pieces of trash to each pair. Place trash cans 20 feet in front of each group. Then space water balloons one

MATERIALS NEEDED:

Water balloons, trash cans, trash.

every three feet in a straight line toward each trash can.

When the leader signals the game to begin, each team will form a wheelbarrow (one partner will stand and hold the feet of the other partner). They will move with the water balloons between them. One at a time, the team must transport the four pieces of trash to the trash can without bursting any water balloons. If a balloon is burst, a piece of trash will be added to that team's small pile. The first team finished wins.

RECOMMENDED GRADES: 1-4

STEWARDSHIP FOR TODAY'S KID

MATERIALS NEEDED:

Chalkboard, chalk.

This activity is meant to teach children about environmental issues and what would be a response that God is happy with. In front of the children, write "Stewardship: Taking Care of God's Stuff." Express to the kids that it is every person's good deed to keep God's world looking good and neat. Use examples like their parents feeling sad if they don't clean their rooms, or get feedback on what they feel inside when they try to make something look good and someone messes it up.

To make your point, use various scenarios. Start each scenario with, "If stewardship is taking care of God's stuff, how can we make God happy in this case?" Then proceed with the following scenarios:

1. You walk to and from school every day. In order to get there, you have to walk through some areas that are very trashy. One day you get tired of all this trash and wish it would all disappear.
2. It is the day before Halloween (mischief night), and your friends are about to go out and toilet paper cars and throw eggs at buses. You did this last year and do not know if you should again.
3. You just learned in class yesterday that aerosol spray cans are bad for the environment. As you are preparing for school, you notice for the first time that your mommy is using an aerosol

spray can for your hair. Is there anything you could say to her?

4. You're walking home from school with a buddy who has just taken a spray can out of his book bag. He wants to spray paint the side of the school building for fun. He begins spraying a design and stops. He gives you the can and pressures you to paint something also.

5. You notice little Mrs. Brown was just planting new plants in the public square for the community. The flowers are very pretty and smell nice. After a while, you notice there is a little girl pulling the flowers up out of the ground one by one. She is laughing and stomping on them right in front of your eyes.

STOP THAT LITTERBUG!

To begin, take the children to any well-traveled area in the neighborhood. If the group is larger than eight, it is best to separate into two teams. Give each team a garbage bag.

The object of this activity is for children to locate someone who is littering and yell, "Stop that litterbug!" When a litterbug is spotted, they must run to pick up the trash as quickly as possible. This activity is deliberate; it often makes the litterbug ashamed of his or her action. This can often reap large bags full.

TIRE DRIVE

When recycling materials, rubber is often overlooked. Have a tire drive where for a week, a month, or a year your group will make a commitment to collect tires left around the community in an effort to beautify the neighborhood. Once the tires are collected, you have the following four options:

1. Do something creative with them. Make tire pottery or use them for an outside group activity.
2. If your city has a rubber recycling center, recycle them.
3. Sell them to a tire dealer.
4. Take them to a legal dump and dispose of them properly.

Provide a way to retrieve tires little kids have located but cannot move. Have a secure place to store them.

RECOMMENDED GRADES: 7-12

TOO MANY AEROSOLS

MATERIALS NEEDED: Five aerosol cans.

Here is a quick activity that can be used either before or after a discussion about aerosols. The purpose of the activity is to overdramatize for young people the toxic effects that aerosols can have in the world. This activity must take place indoors. To begin, give five individuals in your group an aerosol can. These cans should contain a spray of room freshener or cooking oil—nothing that could make the kids sick. Tell the kids to begin at the signal. They must hold the cans facing upward and spray, while seated, for one entire minute. The leader will keep track of time. Be strict about making sure no one is spraying a can toward anyone. All cans should point upward.

When the time is up, your room will often be cloudy and nearly asphyxiating. If necessary, have the group step outside for fresh air until the room clears. When it does, reenter and begin to discuss how aerosols are doing the same thing to our atmosphere. They are literally choking the ozone—the earthly biosphere—and endangering human health.

RECOMMENDED GRADES: 3-7

TRASH ART

Here is a craft idea to use with leftover trash scraps. "Trash Art" is an attempt to encourage young people to use their creativity to build or create some form of artwork as an alternative recycling motivation. Every participant must be given ten pieces of trash. These items should be a mixture of things (bottles, paper, cans, and so on). Be sure all items are cleaned and sanitary. Each individual will also be given glue, four crayons, five pieces of construction paper, and a 15" x 15" cardboard square. These items should be creatively made into an art form the artist will be proud of. Display everything. Have the children explain to the group what they have made and name the abstraction. This is a positive activity that can recycle trash in a different manner.

MATERIALS NEEDED:
Trash scraps, glue, crayons, construction paper, 15" x 15" cardboard squares.

TRASH PARTY CELEBRATION

RECOMMENDED GRADES: All

The purpose here is to plan an afternoon of community awareness activities in which the theme is trash cleanup. This is a great community-building activity.

There are three parts to this activity. Part one is the trash cleanup contest. Gather the entire group and break the group up into teams of ten. Designate a particular area for each team to clean. Hand out trash bags (have reserve trash bags available). Allow one hour for the event to run. Let each team know it is competing against each other to determine who can collect the most trash. When the event is over, have each team report how many filled bags it collected. Add them up, announce the total number, and pile the bags up in trash containers. This will be cause for celebration.

The second part is to celebrate. Set up fun outside activities. Include lots of music, food, recreation, and celebration.

The third part is an awards ceremony to be held during the celebration. An award should be given to the team that collected the most trash. Use this time to also recognize any youths or adults who should be awarded. Once this is over, let the trash party continue.

MATERIALS NEEDED:
Trash bags, food, music.

RECOMMENDED
GRADES:
5-10

TRASHBUSTERS

**MATERIALS
NEEDED:**
Garbage bags.

This is a great service project to do in a housing development. Some nonhigh-rise housing developments have small yards. Often many of them are cluttered with trash that people or the wind has put there. Form a "Trashbusters" team that will, as often as possible, knock on doors and ask for permission to clean up the yard for free. This can be an excellent promotion for your youth group and can often result in new members.

RECOMMENDED
GRADES:
K-6

URBAN POTPOURRI

**MATERIALS
NEEDED:**
Lunch bags.

The purpose of this activity is to sensitize young people to the good smells within their community. Walk around the community picking flowers, plants, or weeds that smell good. These should come from empty lots or sidewalks, not people's yards. Once you have a good number collected, gather some of the harvest in pretty bunches and allow them to dry. To retain the smell, it is best to hang them in bunches indoors. Once dry (which may take a few days), make a mix of the harvest and put bunches in lunch bags for the group members to take home.

CHAPTER 2

MIXERS

Mixer	K	1st	2d	3d	4th	5th	6th	7th	8th	9th	10th	11th	12th
	ELEMENTARY							MIDDLE SCHOOL			HIGH SCHOOL		
BAREFOOT SHOE SEARCH									X	X	X	X	X
BEACH BALL BLITZ							X	X	X	X	X		
COOKIE SORT				X	X	X	X	X	X				
EIGHTY-FIVE				X	X	X	X	X	X				
FOUR CORNERS									X	X	X	X	X
GUESS THE SIGNATURE								X	X	X	X	X	X
HERE I STAND								X	X	X	X	X	X
JAR ME								X	X	X	X	X	X
KWANZAA MIX										X	X	X	X
MY SHIRT, YOUR NAME		X	X	X	X								
PICKPOCKET							X	X	X	X	X	X	X
PUZZLE PLAY						X	X	X	X	X	X	X	X
QUESTION TOSS							X	X	X	X	X	X	X
SHARE SHUFFLE							X	X	X	X	X	X	X
SHARE THE DREAM									X	X	X	X	X
TALENT GUESS							X	X	X	X	X	X	X
TRY TO FIND ME MIXER									X	X	X	X	X
VEHICLE MIX					X	X	X	X					
WANNA BANNA ZOOM							X	X	X	X	X		
WHO-A YOU-A ME-A						X	X	X	X	X	X	X	X
"WHO"DLUM					X	X	X	X	X	X	X		
WHO'S WHO							X	X	X	X	X	X	X
YOU DON'T KNOW?							X	X	X	X			
YOU'RE MY BABY								X	X	X	X	X	X
FOR STAFF ONLY: ROTATION EDUCATION	X	X	X	X	X	X	X	X	X	X	X	X	X

INDOOR GAMES FOR SMALL GROUPS

Game	ELEMENTARY							MIDDLE SCHOOL			HIGH SCHOOL		
	K	1st	2d	3d	4th	5th	6th	7th	8th	9th	10th	11th	12th
CAR PINBALL	X	X	X	X	X	X							
CLUB BY PHONE									X	X	X	X	X
COLOR ME QUICK	X	X	X	X	X								
COUGH, SNIFF, SNEEZE	X	X	X	X	X								
CUP CLASH							X	X	X	X	X	X	X
ELEVATOR RACE								X	X	X	X	X	X
FEUD IT OUT									X	X	X	X	X
FIND THAT TUNE						X	X	X	X	X	X	X	X
FOR CLOSE FRIENDS ONLY										X	X	X	X
HAIR SCARE										X	X	X	X
HIGH CHAIR										X	X	X	X
LAUNDRY FOLDING CONTEST						X	X	X	X	X	X	X	X
MAKE ME SPLASH								X	X	X	X	X	X
MISSING LETTER					X	X	X						
PAINT THE LEADERS	X	X	X	X	X	X	X	X	X	X	X	X	X
PATTY FAKE				X	X	X	X						
PIN THE TAIL ON THE YOUTH WORKER	X	X	X	X									
PUT THE COIN IN THE FUNNEL					X	X	X	X	X	X			
READY, SET, BOUNCE	X	X	X	X									
RHYTHM YOUTH GROUP	X	X	X	X	X	X	X	X	X	X	X	X	X
RUSH THAT NAME				X	X	X	X	X	X	X			
SCATTERGORIES							X	X	X	X	X	X	X
SPY EYE							X	X	X	X			
TOP GUN						X	X	X	X	X			
TURKEY STARE					X	X	X	X	X	X			
THE WANDERER	X	X	X	X	X	X							
WET BACK							X	X	X	X	X	X	X
WHAT'S IT TO YOU?							X	X	X	X	X	X	X
WHITE OUT PAINTINGS			X	X	X	X							

INDOOR GAMES FOR LARGE GROUPS

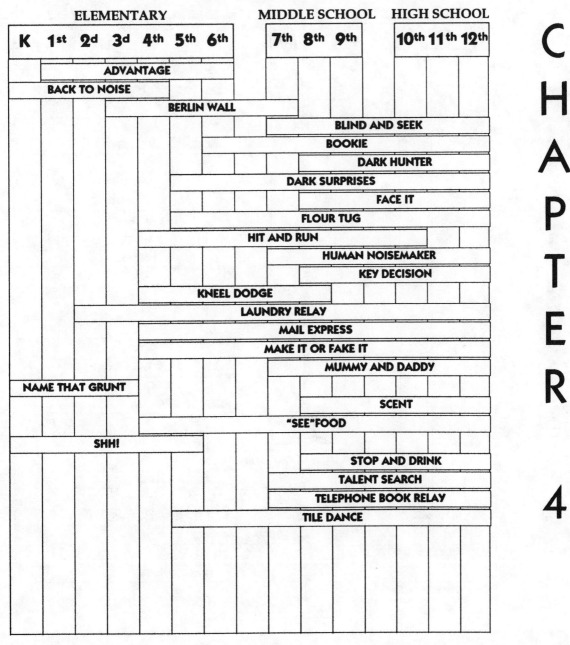

	ELEMENTARY							MIDDLE SCHOOL			HIGH SCHOOL		
	K	1st	2d	3d	4th	5th	6th	7th	8th	9th	10th	11th	12th
ADVANTAGE		●	●	●	●	●	●						
BACK TO NOISE	●	●	●	●	●	●							
BERLIN WALL				●	●	●	●	●					
BLIND AND SEEK								●	●	●	●		
BOOKIE							●	●	●	●			
DARK HUNTER									●	●	●	●	
DARK SURPRISES						●	●	●	●	●			
FACE IT									●	●	●	●	
FLOUR TUG						●	●	●	●	●			
HIT AND RUN					●	●	●	●	●	●			
HUMAN NOISEMAKER								●	●	●	●	●	
KEY DECISION									●	●	●	●	●
KNEEL DODGE					●	●	●	●	●				
LAUNDRY RELAY			●	●	●	●	●	●	●	●	●	●	●
MAIL EXPRESS					●	●	●	●	●	●	●	●	●
MAKE IT OR FAKE IT					●	●	●	●	●	●	●	●	
MUMMY AND DADDY								●	●	●	●	●	●
NAME THAT GRUNT	●	●	●										
SCENT									●	●	●	●	●
"SEE"FOOD								●	●	●			
SHH!	●	●	●	●	●	●	●						
STOP AND DRINK									●	●	●	●	●
TALENT SEARCH								●	●	●	●	●	●
TELEPHONE BOOK RELAY								●	●	●	●	●	●
TILE DANCE					●	●	●	●	●	●	●	●	●

CHAPTER 4

OUTDOOR GAMES FOR SMALL GROUPS

Game	ELEMENTARY							MIDDLE SCHOOL			HIGH SCHOOL		
	K	1st	2d	3d	4th	5th	6th	7th	8th	9th	10th	11th	12th
ANNA BANANA				X	X	X	X	X	X	X	X	X	X
BASKETBALL SPIN CONTEST									X	X	X	X	X
BOTTLE DRAG					X	X	X	X	X	X	X	X	X
CARTRIDGE HORSESHOES			X	X	X	X	X						
CHICKEN EATING CONTEST								X	X	X	X	X	X
DOUBLE DUTCH					X	X	X	X	X	X	X	X	X
DUMPSTER HEAVE										X	X	X	X
EGG IN MOUTH RELAY								X	X	X	X	X	X
FILL THE BUCKET								X	X	X	X	X	
FIND THE AIR HORN					X	X	X	X	X				
HIGH-RISER									X	X	X	X	X
HOBO						X	X	X	X	X	X	X	X
KICK THE BUTT	X	X	X	X	X	X	X	X	X	X	X	X	X
NO DRINKING AT THE BAR											X	X	X
O'CLOCK								X	X	X	X	X	X
OVER THE HEAD TOSS									X	X	X	X	X
PIGEON								X	X	X	X	X	X
PUSH-UP CHALLENGE						X	X	X	X	X	X	X	X
RUG RAT RACE			X	X	X	X	X	X					
ROCK PUT											X	X	X
SHOE TIE FLY			X	X	X	X	X						
SHOOT THE CREAM					X	X	X	X	X	X	X	X	X
SNOW STEPS							X	X	X	X	X	X	X
SQUEEZE THE LEMON					X	X	X	X	X				
SQUIRREL CHASE	X	X	X	X	X								
STEP INTELLIGENCE							X	X	X	X	X	X	X
SUBWAY ADVANCE					X	X	X	X	X				
TICKLE MONSTER	X	X	X	X									
TRACK WHACK						X	X	X	X	X	X	X	X
TUG CHALLENGE	X	X	X	X									
WATER PRESSURE					X	X	X	X	X				

OUTDOOR GAMES FOR LARGE GROUPS

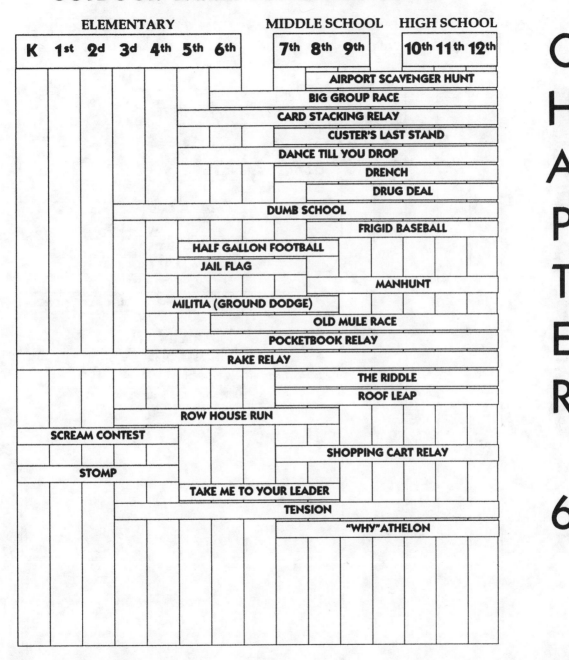

Game	ELEMENTARY							MIDDLE SCHOOL			HIGH SCHOOL		
	K	1st	2d	3d	4th	5th	6th	7th	8th	9th	10th	11th	12th
AIRPORT SCAVENGER HUNT									X	X	X	X	X
BIG GROUP RACE						X	X	X	X	X	X	X	X
CARD STACKING RELAY					X	X	X	X	X	X	X	X	X
CUSTER'S LAST STAND								X	X	X	X	X	X
DANCE TILL YOU DROP								X	X	X	X	X	X
DRENCH										X	X	X	X
DRUG DEAL										X	X	X	X
DUMB SCHOOL				X	X	X	X	X	X	X	X	X	X
FRIGID BASEBALL										X	X	X	X
HALF GALLON FOOTBALL					X	X	X	X	X				
JAIL FLAG					X	X	X	X	X				
MANHUNT									X	X	X	X	X
MILITIA (GROUND DODGE)				X	X	X	X	X	X				
OLD MULE RACE							X	X	X	X	X	X	X
POCKETBOOK RELAY				X	X	X	X	X	X				
RAKE RELAY	X	X	X	X	X	X	X						
THE RIDDLE										X	X	X	X
ROOF LEAP								X	X	X	X	X	X
ROW HOUSE RUN				X	X	X	X	X	X				
SCREAM CONTEST	X	X	X	X									
SHOPPING CART RELAY								X	X	X	X	X	X
STOMP	X	X	X										
TAKE ME TO YOUR LEADER					X	X	X	X	X				
TENSION								X	X	X	X	X	X
"WHY" ATHELON								X	X	X	X	X	X

CHAPTER 6

RELATIONAL ACTIVITIES

Activity	ELEMENTARY							MIDDLE SCHOOL			HIGH SCHOOL		
	K	1st	2d	3d	4th	5th	6th	7th	8th	9th	10th	11th	12th
APPLICATION HELP											X	X	X
BIRTHDAY ADVENTURE			X	X	X	X	X	X	X	X	X	X	X
BUS STOP PRAYERS	X	X	X	X									
BUY A BOOK	X	X	X	X	X	X	X	X	X	X	X	X	X
CLOTHES WASHING FUN	X	X	X	X	X	X	X	X	X	X	X	X	X
CLUBHOUSE CLUB					X	X	X	X					
DAY LOCKUP					X	X	X	X	X	X	X	X	X
GET A LIFE								X	X	X	X	X	X
LUNCH DATE					X	X	X	X	X	X	X	X	X
MAKE A CAMP BROCHURE						X	X	X	X	X	X	X	X
MINISTRY BALL						X	X	X	X	X	X	X	X
MORNING ACCOUNTABILITY GROUP								X	X	X	X	X	X
MUSIC LESSONS	X	X	X	X	X	X	X	X	X	X	X	X	X
OUT FOR THE DAY					X	X	X	X	X	X	X	X	X
PRAYER CHAIN					X	X	X	X	X	X	X	X	X
SPENDING TIME WITH A NOBODY	X	X	X	X	X	X	X	X	X	X	X	X	X
TURNABOUT IS FAIR PLAY					X	X	X	X	X	X	X	X	X

EDUCATIONAL ACTIVITIES

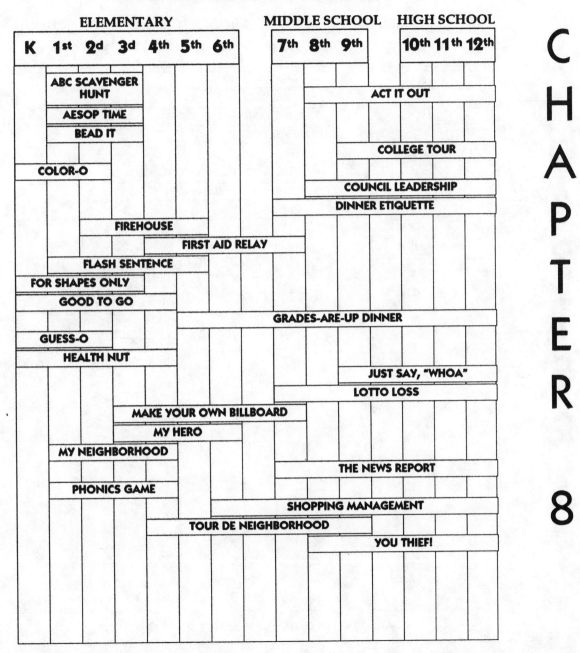

	ELEMENTARY							MIDDLE SCHOOL			HIGH SCHOOL		
K	1st	2d	3d	4th	5th	6th		7th	8th	9th	10th	11th	12th

- ABC SCAVENGER HUNT
- AESOP TIME
- BEAD IT
- COLOR-O
- ACT IT OUT
- COLLEGE TOUR
- COUNCIL LEADERSHIP
- DINNER ETIQUETTE
- FIREHOUSE
- FIRST AID RELAY
- FLASH SENTENCE
- FOR SHAPES ONLY
- GOOD TO GO
- GRADES-ARE-UP DINNER
- GUESS-O
- HEALTH NUT
- JUST SAY, "WHOA"
- LOTTO LOSS
- MAKE YOUR OWN BILLBOARD
- MY HERO
- MY NEIGHBORHOOD
- THE NEWS REPORT
- PHONICS GAME
- SHOPPING MANAGEMENT
- TOUR DE NEIGHBORHOOD
- YOU THIEF!

CHAPTER 8

FAMILY ACTIVITIES

Activity	K	1st	2d	3d	4th	5th	6th	7th	8th	9th	10th	11th	12th
	ELEMENTARY							MIDDLE SCHOOL			HIGH SCHOOL		
ADOPT A KID	X	X	X	X	X	X	X	X	X	X	X	X	X
BABY BOOM	X	X	X	X	X	X	X	X	X	X	X	X	X
FAMILY DISH NIGHT	X	X	X	X	X	X	X	X	X	X	X	X	X
FAMILY EXPENSES					X	X	X	X	X	X	X	X	X
FAMILY WINDOW	X	X	X										
GUESS WHO'S COMING TO VISIT?				X	X	X	X	X	X	X	X	X	X
HEIRLOOM NIGHT						X	X	X	X	X	X	X	X
HOMEBOY	X	X	X	X	X	X	X	X	X	X	X	X	X
MY BLUEPRINT			X	X	X	X	X						
MY MOMMY IS . . .	X	X	X	X	X	X	X						
OLD BUT NOT COLD										X	X	X	X
OUR HERITAGE									X	X	X	X	X
ROLE SWITCH										X	X	X	X
THE VERY FIRST TIME WE MET										X	X	X	X
THIS OLD BLOCK									X	X	X	X	X
WHO IS MY FATHER?										X	X	X	X
FOR PARENTS ONLY: DINNER DATE AND PARENTS' NIGHT OUT	X	X	X	X	X	X	X	X	X	X	X	X	X

CHAPTER 9

POLITICAL ACTIVITIES

	ELEMENTARY							MIDDLE SCHOOL			HIGH SCHOOL		
	K	1st	2d	3d	4th	5th	6th	7th	8th	9th	10th	11th	12th
AIDS REVIVAL					■	■	■	■	■	■	■	■	■
BOYCOTT						■	■	■	■	■	■	■	■
CAP COLLECTION								■	■	■	■	■	■
DON'T TRASH WITH ME								■	■	■			
DRUG PARADE	■	■	■	■	■	■	■	■	■	■	■	■	■
FEMINIST MANIFESTO									■	■	■	■	■
GOD AND GOVERNMENT									■	■	■	■	■
HOMELESSNESS VIDEO									■	■	■	■	■
HOMOSEXUAL AWARENESS									■	■	■	■	■
INJUSTICE GAME		■	■	■	■								
KU KLUX KLAN MARCH									■	■	■	■	
LETTER TO A SOLDIER		■	■	■	■	■	■						
THE MAJORITY DOESN'T ALWAYS WIN							■	■	■	■	■	■	■
MANAGEMENT APPRECIATION DAY	■	■	■	■	■	■	■	■	■	■	■	■	■
MISREPRESENTATION CAMPAIGN								■	■	■	■	■	■
MURDER WALL						■	■	■	■	■	■	■	■
THE OVERGROUND TIMES											■	■	■
PUBLIC SERVICE ANNOUNCEMENT									■	■	■	■	■
RUNNING FOR MAYOR								■	■	■	■	■	■
WHAT IS LIFE?										■	■	■	■

RELIGIOUS ACTIVITIES

	ELEMENTARY							MIDDLE SCHOOL			HIGH SCHOOL		
Activity	K	1st	2d	3d	4th	5th	6th	7th	8th	9th	10th	11th	12th
ALL SAINTS DAY	■	■	■	■	■	■	■						
CHRISTIAN HUNT						■	■	■					
THE CHURCH'S CREED											■	■	■
THE DEVIL CAN'T WIN						■	■	■	■				
EVERY LITTLE STEP I TAKE	■	■	■	■	■	■							
GOD'S BOX						■	■	■	■				
HALLOWEEN HOUSE								■	■	■	■	■	■
I'M A PROPHET				■	■	■	■						
JEHOVAH'S WITNESS VISITS								■	■	■	■	■	■
"RAP"TURE								■	■	■	■		
SCRIPTURE PARAPHRASE											■	■	■
SIN'S POTHOLE									■	■	■	■	■
STEEL MOUNTAIN DEVOTIONS						■	■	■	■	■	■	■	■
WHAT WOULD GOD OR THE DEVIL SAY?	■	■	■	■	■								
WRITE A SERMON								■	■	■	■	■	■
A YOUTH LIBERATION FOR YOUR CHURCH									■	■	■	■	■

CULTURAL ACTIVITIES

	ELEMENTARY							MIDDLE SCHOOL			HIGH SCHOOL		
K	1st	2d	3d	4th	5th	6th		7th	8th	9th	10th	11th	12th

ART IN MUSIC

BIG . . .

FASHION EXTRAVAGANZA

I AM LIKE . . .

IDENTIFYING *KWANZAA*

IT'S A CULTURAL THING YOU WOULDN'T UNDERSTAND

JESUS IS LIKE ME

KNOW THYSELF

KWANZAA SCRAMBLE

MALE RESPONSIBILITY TEST

MARTIN/MALCOLM DEBATE

MUSIC OF MY CULTURE

MY COMPLEXION, YOUR COMPLEXION

MY HAIR, YOUR HAIR

OUR NEIGHBORHOOD HEROES

RACIAL UNDERSTANDING CLUB

WHAT'S IN A NAME?

ENVIRONMENTAL ACTIVITIES

Activity	K	1st	2d	3d	4th	5th	6th	7th	8th	9th	10th	11th	12th
	ELEMENTARY							**MIDDLE SCHOOL**			**HIGH SCHOOL**		
BIG GROUP RECYCLING CHALLENGE	X	X	X	X	X	X	X	X	X	X	X	X	X
BUILD A TRASH BOX								X	X	X	X	X	X
ENDANGERED SPECIES GAME							X	X	X	X	X	X	X
ENVIRONMENTAL MURAL							X	X	X	X	X	X	X
ENVIRONMENTAL STUDY			X	X	X	X	X	X	X	X	X	X	X
FIELD CLEANUP						X	X	X	X	X	X	X	X
GARDEN PLANTING			X	X	X	X	X	X	X	X			
I CAN			X	X	X	X	X						
MUD POTTERY		X	X	X	X	X	X						
NOISE POLLUTION SOLUTION							X	X	X	X	X	X	X
PLANTING IN FAITH	X	X	X	X	X	X	X						
RECYCLING CAMPAIGN	X	X	X	X	X	X	X	X	X	X			
STEWARDSHIP FOR TODAY'S KID		X	X	X	X	X	X						
SPLASH OR TRASH								X	X	X	X	X	X
STOP THAT LITTERBUG!	X	X	X	X									
TIRE DRIVE			X	X	X	X	X	X	X	X	X	X	X
TOO MANY AEROSOLS								X	X	X	X	X	X
TRASH ART				X	X	X	X	X	X	X			
TRASH PARTY CELEBRATION	X	X	X	X	X	X	X	X	X	X	X	X	X
TRASHBUSTERS					X	X	X	X	X	X	X	X	X
URBAN POTPOURRI	X	X	X	X	X	X	X